How to use this book

What do you mean how to use this book? It's a book for fi s sake.
Well yes, you are right, kinda.

There are 5 common core emails that almost every business sends out
to on-board users.
As you read this book and see the examples from each company, fill out
each section of the work sheet. Write in the ideas and wording that you
believe will work well for your own audience.
At the end of the book you should have a strong on boarding plan to
convert more customers in just 30 days.

Download the worksheet here:
http://audiencestack.com/static/book-30-days-to-sell-worksheet.html

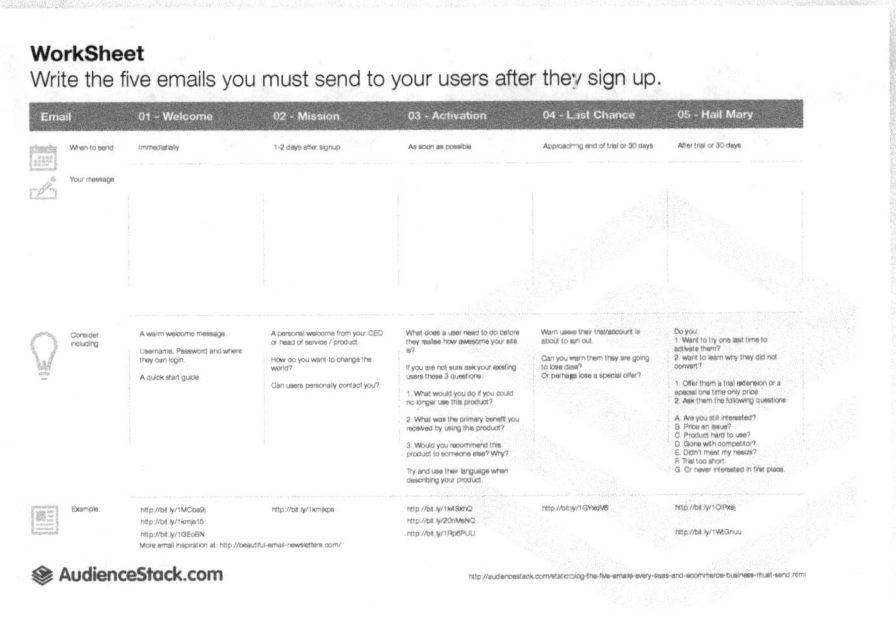

Underpants Gnomes

One of the greatest business and marketing lessons from South Park, the animated Comedy Central show from Trey Stone and Matt Parker, is where a bunch of gnomes steal underpants from the townsfolk based on the following business model:
- Step 1. Collect underpants
- Step 2. -
- Step 3. Profit

while singing a Disney-like happy tune.

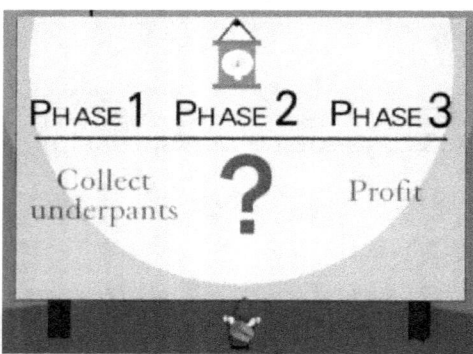 

When asked about step two, the gnomes stare blankly because obviously step three:profit is the important step.
See it here: http://beautiful-email-newsletters.com/underpants-gnomes/

Too many companies today work on exactly this model.
- Step 1. Collect sign ups
- Step 2. -
- Step 3. Profit

Then they look around confused when the profit does not materialise. Successful companies know that the selling starts after sign up. Step 2 needs to help, prompt and encourage users, while continuing to sell the benefits of the product or service, right up to the point users hand over their credit card; and in many cases beyond.

Collected here are the automated 30 day email campaigns of the world's leading Saas, e-commerce and service companies, picked apart and analysed to help you put together your own user activation campaigns. Read on to see how these companies convert users from try to buy.

30

DAYS

TO SELL

Converting users from try to buy!

Proven automated sign-up campaigns
from the world's leading web companies

Alan O'Rourke

Contents

The key activation metric

Twitter.com knows that a new user needs to follow 30 users before they understand value of the service and stick around to use it. This is the core metric that activates a user. So the initial emails from Twitter push a user to follow 30 users. Facebook adopts a similar approach.

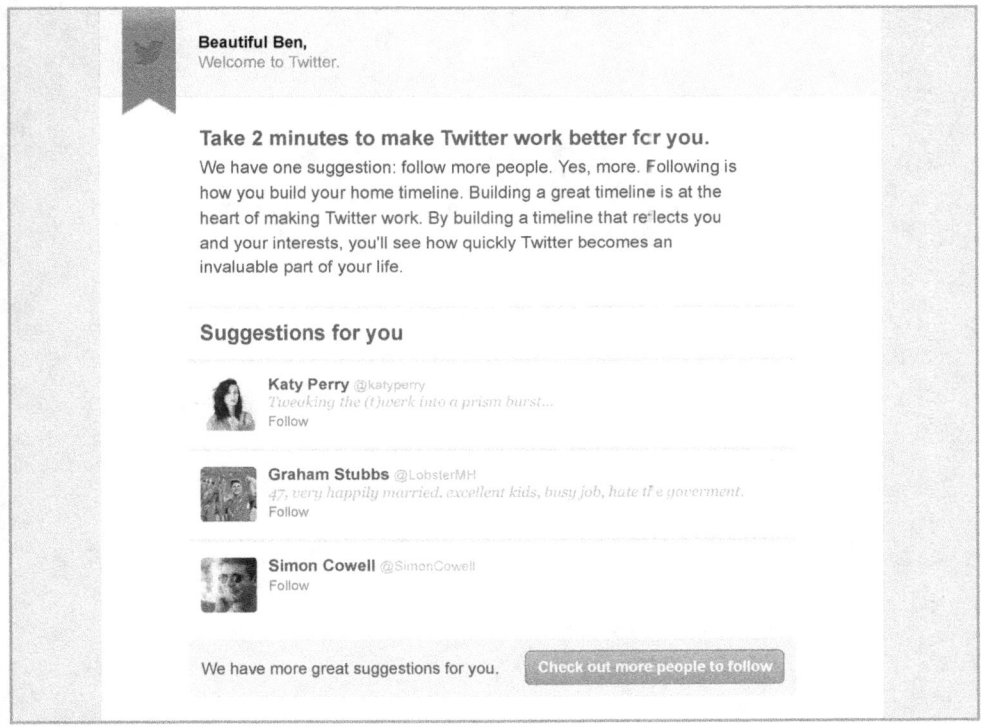

For Dropbox.com, the file backup and syncing service, the key activation metric is installing their desktop app. While online fashion retailers like Zuilily, Scoutmob and Fab.com know that a user needs to buy something early, however small.

E-commerce sites like Fab.com know a user needs to buy something early, however small

With that in mind they offer a coupon code in their welcome mails. Other e-commerce sites open with some kind of sale, preferably with a time limit to prompt users to buy. The best time to send these offers is immediately when a user signs up as that is the point a user is most engaged with the site and brand.

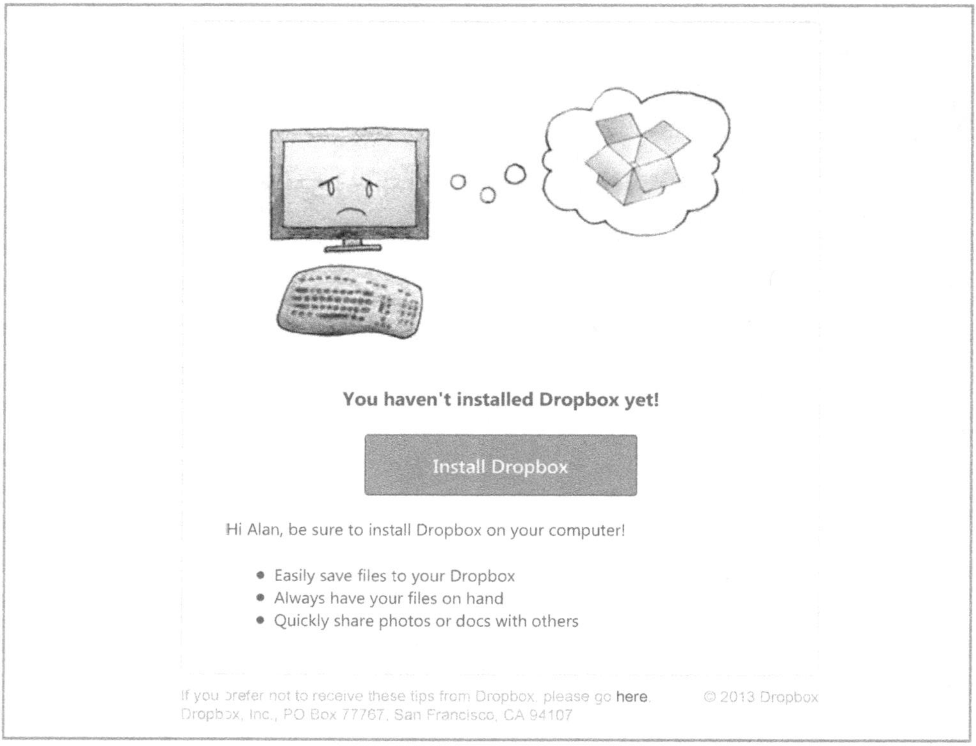

You haven't installed Dropbox yet!

Install Dropbox

Hi Alan, be sure to install Dropbox on your computer!

- Easily save files to your Dropbox
- Always have your files on hand
- Quickly share photos or docs with others

If you prefer not to receive these tips from Dropbox, please go here.   © 2013 Dropbox
Dropbox, Inc., PO Box 77767, San Francisco, CA 94107

Dave McClure, prominent investor and founding partner of the San Francisco business incubator 500 start ups highlights this in his *Startup Metrics for Pirates* framework: AARRR!!

Customer Lifecycle: 5 Steps to Success
- **A** cquisition: users come to the site from various channels
- **A ctivation: users enjoy 1st visit: "happy" user experience**
- **R** etention: users come back, visit site multiple times
- **R** eferral: users like product enough to refer others
- **R** evenue: users conduct some monetization behavior

AARRR!

For Dave activation emails are a simple and easy feature and in his experience setting the emails to go out 3, 7 & 30 days after a user signs up is a good starting point.

eBay and Facebook's growth teams work to a similar and very simple framework of things to measure and improve on.
- Acquisition – Get the right people in front of your product
- **Activation – Provide a great initial experience**
- Engagement – Keep users engaged and deliver value
- Virality – Get people to recommend your product

The order of these steps may vary but activation is the critical link between aquisition and revenue

Sean Ellis of Qualaroo (and formally Dropbox) recommends you need to identify the must-have experience of your product and to look for ways to front-load that experience. The sooner your prospects experience the value of your product the better. In the case of Twitter for example, the must have experience is finding out what your friends or people you are interested in are doing and talking about. And having enough people to keep your twitter stream new and updated every time you read it.

Sometime the easiest way to find out is to ask your users. Surveys and customer development can help you to identify what the must-have experience means for your product so try survey questions like the following.

Survey users to find your key activation metric

1. What would you do if you could no longer use this product?

2. What was the primary benefit you received by using this product?

3. Would you recommend this product to someone else? Why?

I worked with Sean on this question for an early stage startup of mine. He developed a survey tool with Kissmetrics (http://survey.io) . The results were amazing for our team and informed not just the activation flow of current users but how we positioned the product in the market to attract customers into the sales funnel.

The $6,000 email

Patrick McKenzie (https://training.kalzumeus.com/) has a great example of how one activation email generated an additional $6,000 for his company.

Patrick runs a business called Appointment Reminder. It does appointment reminder phone calls/SMS messages/emails to the clients. The key activation metric for Appointment Rem nder is "Has the user scheduled more than 5 appointments?" With that metric Patrick can quickly see which trial users are going to cancel at the end of the month because they have not set enough reminders. As he says

"Anything I can do to decrease the number of cancellations prints money."

So Patrick started mailing users at day 20 of their trial. If they had already hit the key activation metric the mail praised them for how much value they had created for their own business. The email also pushed how great the value of Appointment Reminder now offered.
If the user had not hit the activation metric they got a rescue email asking how Patrick can help and if the user needs more time. Just one of these emails, to a user who had never set up a reminder resulted in an enterprise sale of $6,000. Here is the email:

```
Hiya [CUSTOMER NAME ELIDED FOR PRIVACY],
Thanks for signing up for the free trial of
Appointment Reminder! We wanted to check in and
see how things are going.

I run a small business myself, so I know things
occasionally get busy. The computer says that
you have scheduled less than a handful of
appointments in Appointment Reminder so far.
You've still got about 10 days left on your free
trial, but we wanted to get in touch to see if we
could help.

We've got two questions for you, if you'd care to
answer:
```

1) Do you just need a bit more time? That is totally OK. We're happy to extend your trial by another month. Send me an email and I can set this up for you.

2) Did you have any trouble getting started with Appointment Reminder? I'd love to hear what we could do to make that easier for you. I'm also happy to walk you through how to set up your reminders / settings / etc over email if you'd like me to.

Do you have any questions? I'm always happy to answer them. My direct email is patrick@appointmentreminder.org -- feel free to email me at any time.

Regards,
Patrick McKenzie

Founder
Appointment Reminder

P.S. A bit of bookkeeping: your free trial will run until [DATE ELIDED FOR PRIVACY]. We'll bill your credit card one day in advance of that, to make sure your service is not interrupted.

30 days and counting...

You have 30 days to convert a user to a paying customer starting NOW. The clock is ticking. What will you do?

The following pages collect and analyse the messaging and strategy companies use to convert trial users to customers in the most important 30 days after sign-up. Each company's strategy is broken down and presented in an easy to understand, single page, visual guide.
You can dig into individual emails on subsequent pages to see how users are prompted to action.

What ever type of online business you run, saas, e-commerce, consulting, read, analyze, and take note of what approach would work for your company and turn your users from try to buy.

SugarSync
File syncing software 30-day trial

 From: SugarSync Customer Support
<no-reply@sugarsync.com>
Date: Thu, Mar 21 at 6:25 PM
Subject: Welcome to SugarSync

01
02
03

04 **From:** SugarSync Customer Support
<no-reply@sugarsync.com>
Date: Sun, Mar 24 at 10:07 AM
Subject: Reminder: Complete your
SugarSync setup now

05
06
07
08
09
10

 From: SugarSync Customer Support
<no-reply@sugarsync.com>
Date: Sun, Mar 31 at 10:58 AM
Subject: Final Reminder: Complete your
SugarSync setup now

11
12
13
14
15
16
17
18
19
20

21 **From:** SugarSync <news@sugarsync.com>
Date: Wed, Apr 10 at 5:00 PM
Subject: SugarSync Mobile Apps Are Free

22
23
24
25
26
27
28

 Monthly newsletter
From: SugarSync <news@sugarsync.com>
Date: Thu, Apr 18 at 1:17 AM
Subject: SugarSync Newsletter: New iOS,
2.0, and more

29
30
31

30 Days To Sell - Converting users from try to buy.

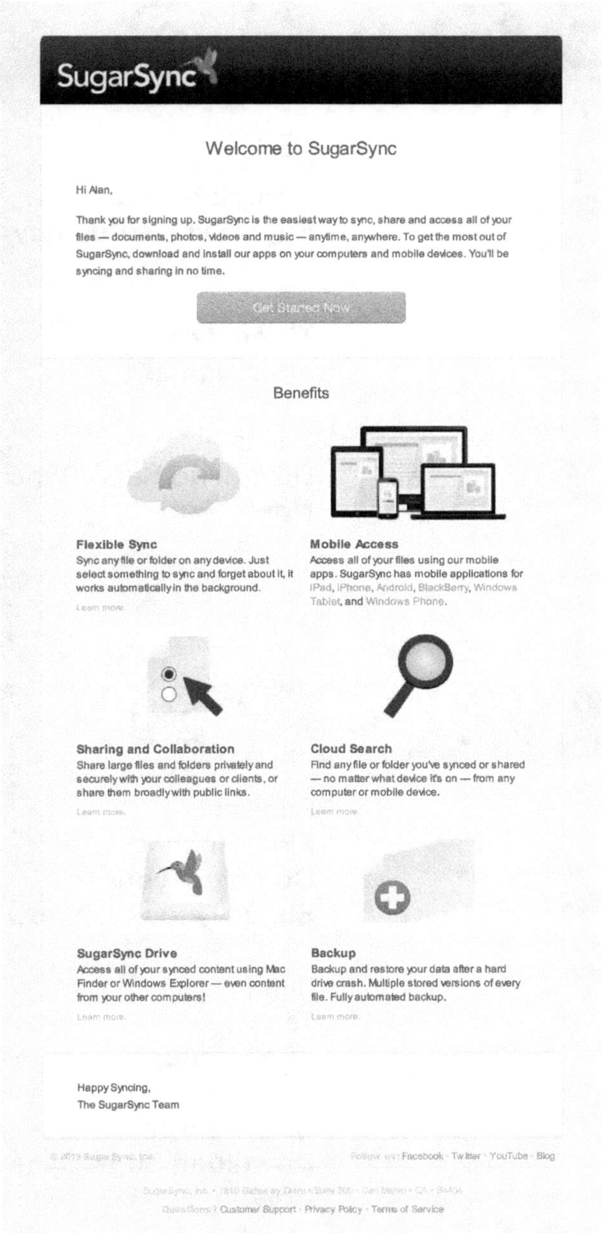

SugarSync

Welcome to SugarSync

Hi Alan,

Thank you for signing up. SugarSync is the easiest way to sync, share and access all of your files — documents, photos, videos and music — anytime, anywhere. To get the most out of SugarSync, download and install our apps on your computers and mobile devices. You'll be syncing and sharing in no time.

Get Started Now

Benefits

Flexible Sync
Sync any file or folder on any device. Just select something to sync and forget about it, it works automatically in the background.
Learn more.

Mobile Access
Access all of your files using our mobile apps. SugarSync has mobile applications for iPad, iPhone, Android, BlackBerry, Windows Tablet, and Windows Phone.

Sharing and Collaboration
Share large files and folders privately and securely with your colleagues or clients, or share them broadly with public links.
Learn more.

Cloud Search
Find any file or folder you've synced or shared — no matter what device it's on — from any computer or mobile device.
Learn more.

SugarSync Drive
Access all of your synced content using Mac Finder or Windows Explorer — even content from your other computers!
Learn more.

Backup
Backup and restore your data after a hard drive crash. Multiple stored versions of every file. Fully automated backup.
Learn more.

Happy Syncing,
The SugarSync Team

© 2012 SugarSync, Inc.   Follow us: Facebook · Twitter · YouTube · Blog

SugarSync, Inc. · 1810 Gateway Drive · Suite 200 · San Mateo · CA · 94404
Questions | Customer Support · Privacy Policy · Terms of Service

---

Subject:
Welcome to SugarSync

Sent:
Immediately

Call to action:
Get started now

 SugarSync are still selling the benefits even though a user has just signed up.

Subject:
Reminder:
**Complete your
SugarSync setup now**

Sent:
**Three days
after signup**

Call to action:
**Download SugarSync
Now**

Subject:
**Final Reminder:
Complete your
SugarSync setup now**

Sent:
**Ten days
after signup**

Call to action:
**Download SugarSync
Now**

30 Days To Sell - Converting users from try to buy.

Subject:
**SugarSync
Mobile Apps Are Free**

Sent:
**Twenty days
after signup**

Call to action
Download now

30 Days To Sell - Converting users from try to buy.

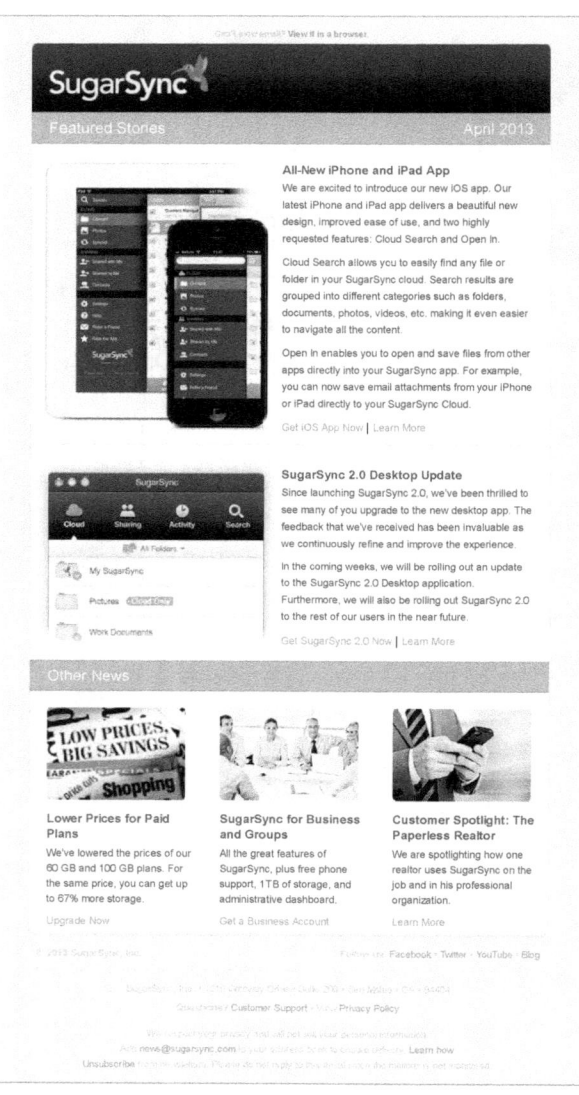

Monthly Newsletter

Subject:
SugarSync Mobile Apps Are Free

Sent:
Twenty eight days after signup

Content:
New features Customer spotlight

30 Days To Sell - Converting users from try to buy.

A warm welcome

First impressions are important. Your first email sets the tone of your relationship and is a deciding factor in whether your subsequent emails, no matter how good, get read by your users.
The welcome email must walk the delicate line between getting a user to do enough to see the value of your business, without asking too much and causing your email to be filed away for reading later (or never).

Compare the minimal, functional approach of Cliniko to bright and visual Asana who try to get you excited about the next steps.

 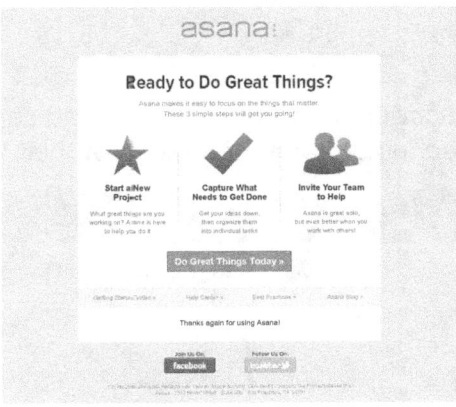

Bug tracking software Fogbugz.com tells you upfront what to expect over your trial to get you looking forward to their emails.

"Over the next six weeks I am going to send you exactly three emails. That's it. I just want to help you learn a bit more about FogBugz."

A welcome email most likely contains the users account information and will be referred to often. So a reminder to save the email with links to contact us, support and helpful guides like Squarespace.com is a good idea to help users.

Some companies like Mailchimp do two emails on sign up. One is your

Welcome to Squarespace

Your 14 day free trial starts today. Here is some important information about your new account. You should save this email, so you can refer to it later.

account information. A second separate welcome mail starts you on a series of 9 how-to guides of their key functionality.

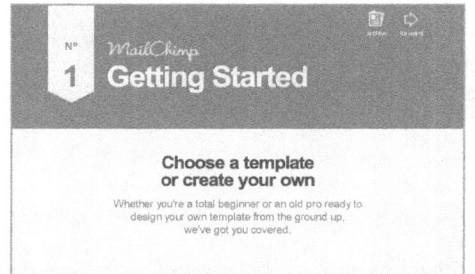

It is very easy to forget how effective the personal approach can be. Clinic booking site WhatClinic.com assign every new user a dedicated account manager so every mail comes from a real person, with a profile picture and signature. Likewise, e-commerce software Shopify.com (p.10) provide a user with their own guru to help. Print company Moo. com give their automated mails a personality called LittleMoo which gives a normal transactional email a sense of fun.

```
"Hello Alan
I'm Little MOO - the bit of software that will be
managing your order with moo.com. It will shortly be
sent to Big MOO, our print machine who will print it
for you in the next few days. I'll let you know when
it's done and on its way to you.
Thanks,
Little MOO, Print Robot"
```

Shopify

E-commerce software, online store builder 14-day trial

 From: Shopify <mailer@shopify.com>
Date: Thu, Mar 21 at 6:19 PM
Subject: Welcome to Shopify

 day after sign-up

02

03

04

05

06

07

08

09

10

11

12

13 **From:** Shopify <mailer@shopify.com>
Date: Tue, Apr 2 at 9:27 AM
14 **Subject:** Your online store is about to close

 **From:** Shopify <mailer@shopify.com>
Date: Thu, Apr 4 at 6:35 AM
Subject: Your online store has closed

15 **Monthly Newsletter**
From: Shopify Newsletter
16 <newsletter@shopify.com>
Date: Thu, Apr 4 at 10:18 PM
17 **Subject:** Get more online sales in April

18

19

20

21

22

23

24

25

26

27

28

29

30

31

30 Days To Sell - Converting users from try to buy.

Welcome to Shopify!  shopify

You've taken the first step towards world domination! Below you will find all of your account information, keep it in a safe place:

Your Store: http://beautifulben.myshopify.com

Your store is currently password protected using the password "droosk". You can remove the password protection when you're ready to launch your store.

Your Store's Admin Area: http://beautifulben.myshopify.com/admin/

If you ever forget your password, you can always recover it by clicking here.

Get ready for some sales!

We've built a step-by-step tutorial into your Store Admin to get you started. You can do the tutorial steps in any order, or skip them completely, it's up to you.

Add Products

Customize Your Design

Add Content

Getting Paid

Setting Taxes

Shipping Settings

Domain Names

Meet your Shopify Guru!

We also provide every store owner with a personal Shopify Guru to help you make your store a success. Your Guru, Alex, can be reached via email at

alex.richards@shopify.com

Alex is available from Monday to Friday from 9am to 5pm EST.

The Shopify Guru Team

SUPPORT | FORUMS | THEME STORE | APP STORE | SHOPIFY EXPERTS | BLOG

© Shopify | 126 York Street, Ottawa, ON, K1N 5T5

Subject:
Welcome to Shopify

Sent:
Immediately

Call to action:
Get ready for some sales

 Shopify have one of the nicer designed email sequences. It is great how they introduce your personal account manager Alex and devote a full third of the email to it. They sell the benefits along with the next steps they want you to take.

30 Days To Sell - Converting users from try to buy.

Your store is about to close!

Hey beautifulben,

Your free Shopify trial will expire in less than 2 days! If you don't want your online store to be closed, please log in and pick a plan. If you have forgotten your password, you can easily recover it here.

Which Plan is Best for You?

Our friendly Sales Team would be happy to help you find the perfect plan for beautifulben. You can reach them by phone (1-888-SHOPIFY) or use our Sales Contact Form.

Get $100 in Credits Today

Pick a plan today and we'll give $100 in free credit for Google AdWords. You can use this to get customers to your online store.

Need Some Help?

Your Shopify Guru, Alex, is standing by to help you get your site up and running and an be reached via email at:

alex.richards@shopify.com

Alex is available from Monday to Friday from 9am to 5pm EST.

The Shopify Guru Team

SUPPORT | FORUMS | THEME STORE | APP STORE | SHOPIFY EXPERTS | BLOG

© Shopify | 126 York Street, Ottawa, ON, K1N 5T5

Subject:
Your online store is about to close

Sent:
Twelve days after signup.

Call to action:
Buy today & get $100 google adwords credits.

Again Shopify reinforce the personal touch. You can phone and chat about what plan you should buy. Shopify know the power of real people.

15

Subject:
Your online store has closed

Sent:
Fourteen days after signup

Call to action:
Re-open your store by picking a plan

 I like the extra hook of saying they have not yet deleted your data. The fear of losing something is a much more powerful driver of behaviour than the want to get something.

Monthly Newsletter

Subject:
Get more online sales in April

Sent:
Fourteen days after signup

Content
Business & marketing advice
Sell more in April
Learning resources
Free 24x7 support
Join our community
Our best blog posts
Try our theme store

---

shopify

Start selling more in April

Dear Alan O'Rourke,

Learning how to launch and grow your online store *can* be challenging. But it doesn't have to be! This month we're excited to announce the launch of Ecommerce University – a free resource to help you grow your business. We'll also tell you about our increased support coverage, pass on some great advice from our forums, and share two of this month's most popular themes.

Learn how to sell more online

Our freshly launched Ecommerce University is a collection of advice on how to sell online. You'll find ebooks, articles, videos, and discussion forums full of tips and tricks for beginners to experts alike – and it's all free.

Check out the new Ecommerce University.

Ecommerce University

Talk to us for free 24x7

We've expanded our customer service capacity to make sure you have the support you need, whenever you need it. Shopify gurus are always available to take your call or answer your email 24 hours a day, 7 days a week.

We also have toll-free and local phone numbers for:

UK: 0800 808 5233
Australia: 03 8400 4750
New Zealand: 07 788 6026
North America: 1 888 746 7439

The best of the forum

Our discussion forums are a place where you can ask questions and connect with other store owners. Here are some of this month's best conversations:

- How to price plus sized clothes
- Opinions on product prices
- Do I need a photographer?
- How do you get rid of old inventory?
- How to verify your Shopify website on Pinterest
- TV advertising: does anyone do it?
- Best tips for social media marketing

The best of the Shopify Blog

Our blog is filled with articles to help you build your business and sell more. Here are some of the most popular blog posts from the past month:

- New Shopify Apps to Help You Sell More
- 10 Must Know Image Optimization Tips
- All About US Trademarks
- Best of the Build-A-Business Mentor Tips

BEST *of the blog* shopify

---

30 Days To Sell - Converting users from try to buy.

Cliniko
Medical Practice Management Software 30-day trial

 From: Cliniko <support@cliniko.com>
Date: Tue, Mar 26 at 4:24 PM
Subject: Welcome to Cliniko!

 01

02

03

 04 **From:** Jim Sadusky <support@cliniko.com>
Date: Fri, Mar 29 at 4:30 PM
05 **Subject:** Need help with Cliniko?

06

07

08

09

10

11

12

13

14

15

16

17

18

19

20

21

 22 **Monthly Newsletter**
From: Cliniko <info@cliniko.com>
23 **Date:** Tue, Apr 16 at 6:28 AM
Subject: Cliniko News - April 2013
24

 From: Cliniko <support@cliniko.com>
Date: Thu, Apr 18 at 5:36 PM
Subject: Cliniko - 7 days of free trial left 25

26

27

28

29

30

31 **From:** support@cliniko.com
Date: Thu, Apr 25 at 5:43 PM
Subject: Cliniko subscription ended

30 Days To Sell - Converting users from try to buy.

Welcome to Cliniko

Hi Alan,

Thanks for signing up for your free trial of Cliniko.

We know you are probably keen to get started right away, so here are the key details you need.

Sign in to your account:

https://beautifulben.cliniko.com/

Username (your email address):

alanresearch36@gmail.com

To get started, we recommend you jump into the settings page and set up the following items.

- Users & Practitioners - Add any other people from your practice that will need access
- Billable Items - Set the prices for any products or services you charge for
- Appointment Types - Add the different types of appointments you service

If you need any help, you can easily get in touch with us at support@cliniko.com, we are happy to help.

Enjoy!

The Cliniko Team
http://www.cliniko.com

Subject:
Welcome to Cliniko!

Sent:
Immediately

Call to action
Set up your clinic

Subject:
Need help with Cliniko?

Sent:
Three days after signup

Call to action:
Contact us. We are real & here to help.

 The personal touch from Jim helps this email seem genuine and helpful.

30 Days To Sell - Converting users from try to buy.

 Cliniko

Cliniko News - April 2013

Hi Everyone,

It's time for another update!

Firstly, we've had Matt Jones join our team a few weeks ago. Matt is a devops and will be spending his time making sure Cliniko is reliable and fast. He has some big plans for infrastructure improvements and we'll announce more as we get closer. Matt's addition brings the Cliniko team up to 8 now. You can read a bit more about Matt here http://www.cliniko.com/blog/238/matt-has-joined-the-cliniko-team/.

We've also been really hard at work on developing new features and improving existing ones. Further below you'll see a list of the main changes we've released in the last couple of months, but really it's nothing compared to what's coming. These are the big 3 that we are currently working on (click the links to see the previews):

- Letter Writing - https://support.cliniko.com/entries/20182502-Letters-to-patients
- Xero Integration - https://support.cliniko.com/entries/20246531-Integration-with-accounting-packages
- iCal Integration - https://support.cliniko.com/entries/20236242-iCal-Integration

We are getting much closer on all of those and can't wait to release them.

On top of all the changes coming out, we also have many new businesses signing up to use Cliniko every day. There have now been over 2 million appointments created in Cliniko and over 1 million patients. We are humbled and thankful for everyones support and it motivates us even further to keep delivering for you all.

Thanks!

Joel Friedlaender
Founder - Cliniko

Recent Changes

Practitioners can view their own revenue reports (01-March-2013)

We made a change so that practitioners can access the practitioner revenue reports, for themselves only.

Contacts (09-March-2013)

We added **Contacts** into Cliniko. This is used to store the details of anyone that isn't a patient. This could be used for other practitioners, suppliers, insurers or anyone else really.

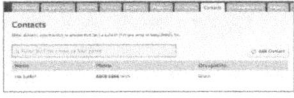

Changes to treatment note autosaving (14-March-2013)

We made a change to treatment note autosaving. This was to allow it to work even if your internet dropped out and a few other benefits too. This change has however been met with mixed reviews, you can see the details and discussion here https://support.cliniko.com/entries/21650900-Big-improvements-to-treatment-note-autosaving. We have more improvements planned for this change.

Security updates (19-March-2013)

We released a few security updates to ensure our security stays top notch and is up to date with current threats.

Improvements to data importing (04-April-2013)

We made some big improvements to data imports. It no longer struggles with large import files and it also lets you "undo" your data imports within 48 hours of importing. You can see your historical imports too.

Stay up to date

Subscribe here:
Cliniko updates and changes

Like our facebook page:
Cliniko facebook page

Follow us on twitter:
@cliniko

Monthly newsletter

Subject:
Cliniko News - April 2013

Sent:
Twenty one days after signup.

Content:
**Letter from the founder
New staff (we are growing)
System updates & new features**

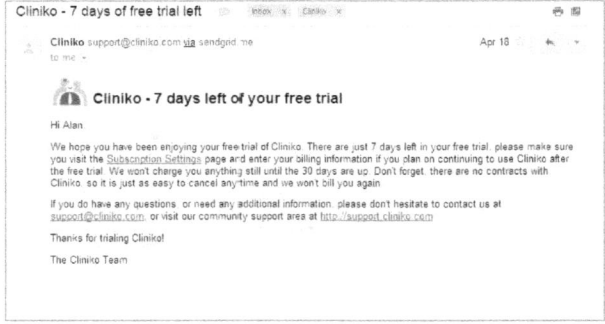

Subject:
Cliniko - 7 days of free trial left

Sent:
Twenty three days after signup.

Call to action:
Add your credit card for uninterrupted service.

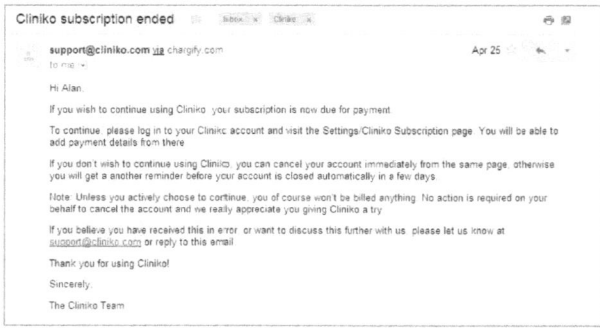

Subject:
Cliniko subscription ended

Sent:
Thirty days after signup.

Call to action:
**Times up.
To continue, log in and add payment details.**

A great series of mails but Cliniko undermine the message and power of this mail. They say time is up and pay now. Then say, oh hang on, you still have a few days. I am lazy so I will hang on for a few more days.

It's common to follow up after a few days with a last, last chance mail or even a special offer. A hail mary email it is called. But best not to worn users it is coming.

30 Days To Sell - Converting users from try to buy.

The step by step course

A great strategy is to take your existing marketing and support content into a step by step 'get started' guide.

A common approach is a list of getting started links in your initial welcome mail, like Shopify in the image on the right. But why miss out on the opportunity of contacting users more often.

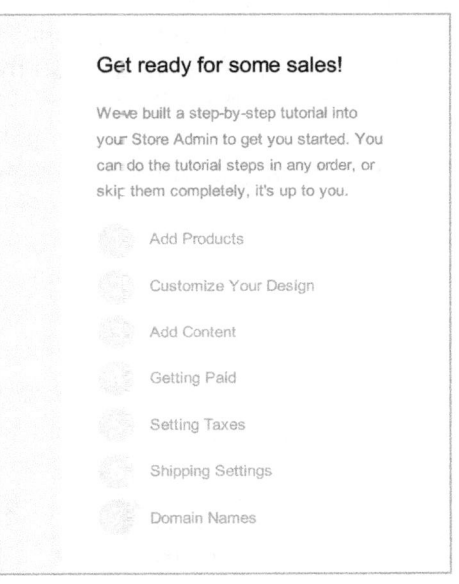

Get ready for some sales!

We've built a step-by-step tutorial into your Store Admin to get you started. You can do the tutorial steps in any order, or skip them completely, it's up to you.

Add Products

Customize Your Design

Add Content

Getting Paid

Setting Taxes

Shipping Settings

Domain Names

A step by step guide gives you a great excuse to regularly contact users to nudge them deeper into your product.

MailChimp go all out with a magnificent nine step guide over the 30 days. At the end of the trial, the user will not only know how to use the application but will feel like a power user.

There are two key benefits.
1. You show your user how to use your application, most especially the key activation features (See the chapter: Core activation metric).

2. You get to contact the user often over the time of the trial. You are helping them out and keeping your business in their mind.

Keep selling the benefits.
It is very easy to get caught up in features with this approach which is a mistake. Features are what you ask your designers and engineers to provide. Benefits are what you hook customers with.
Facebook, for example, do not talk about the ability to easily import all your email contacts from Gmail (feature). Instead they talk about how easy it is to connect with all your friends (benefit). Shopify, in the image above, lead with the the benefit of getting more sales.

The great thing is you probably have this content already.

- Read your support queries for the most common issues people have and grab your replies.
- Take your marketing material and break it down into easy guides.
- Focus on the key activation metric (See the chapter: Core activation metric) and push it early.
- Take the reports from your sales team and user testing teams and grab the most common questions and answers.

30 Days To Sell - Converting users from try to buy.

An additional benefit of this approach is that you are preempting support issues which make you look great to prospective customers, while at the same time cutting your support costs.

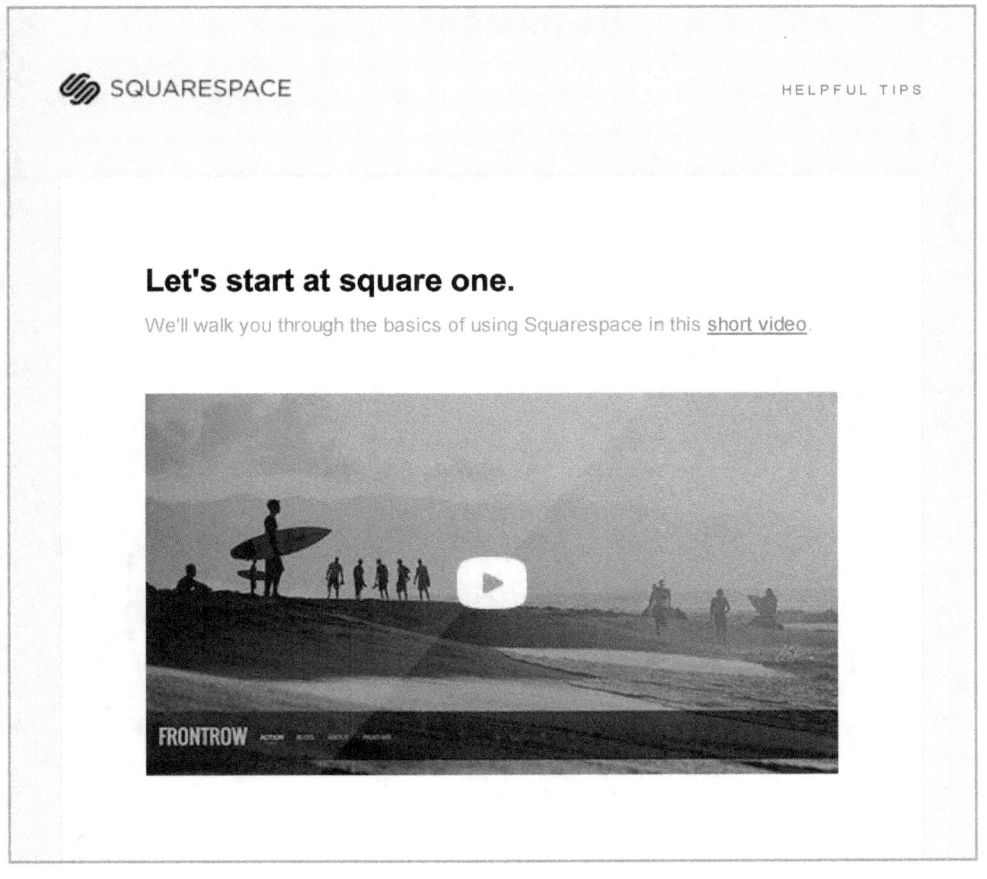

How you present your guides is up to you and your audience. Shutterstock present simple, but visual, introductions to their main features and benefits while Squarespace deliver a more indepth video guide to the user. Basecamp from 37Signals opt for a more interactive 30 minute Webinar or live class to quickly teach a user how to become a Basecamp pro.

Hey Alan,

You should join us for a live, online class that quickly teaches you and your team how to become Basecamp Pros in just 30 minutes.

You'll get filled in on every key feature in Basecamp, see examples of how we run our projects here at 37signals, and we'll do live Q&A just for you and your team to boot.

Best of all, Basecamp classes are free!

9 Out Of 10 Attendees Feel More Comfortable Using Basecamp After Attending Basecamp Classes

Here's what some of them had to say...

"It was really perfect for a first webinar on Basecamp, just enough to get functional and get the toes in the water...THANKS, Basecamp ROCKS!"

"I was happy it was only 30 minutes. Lots of good info packed in. It's hard to allot 60 minutes to a webinar. Your staff comes across as extremely customer centric and eager to assist! I've only been using Basecamp for 2 weeks but LOVE it so far. Thanks for all you do and have a great day!"

"Nice work. I used basecamp classic for many years. This was a good way to get a feel for the new version. Thanks so much!"

Hurry, space is limited and classes fill up quickly.

Register today to save your spot

From the team that proudly brings you Basecamp, 37signals

P.S. Know anyone on your team that should sign up? Be sure to let

AnyMeeting
Web conference solution 30-day trial

From: AnyMeeting
<noreply@anymeeting.com>
Date: Thu, Mar 21 at 5:50 PM
Subject: Welcome to AnyMeeting - Get Started

01
02
03
04

05
From: AnyMeeting
<noreply@anymeeting.com>
Date: Mon, Mar 25 at 5:51 PM
Subject: Lesson 1 - How to Run a Meeting

06
07

Monthly newsletter
From: AnyMeeting
<noreply@anymeeting.com>
Date: Thu, Mar 28 at 9:49 PM
Subject: Newsletter: New iPad App + 10 Easy Marketing Tips for Branding Your Small Biz

08
09
From: AnyMeeting
<noreply@anymeeting.com>
Date: Fri, Mar 29 at 5:51 PM
Subject: Lesson #2: Video Calls and Screen Sharing

10
11
12

13
From: AnyMeeting
<noreply@anymeeting.com>
Date: Tue, Apr 2 at 6:51 PM
Subject: Lesson 3: Scheduling Meetings

14
15
16
17
18

19
From: AnyMeeting
<noreply@anymeeting.com>
Date: Mon, Apr 8 at 6:51 PM
Subject: Lesson 4: Promote

20
21
22
23
24
25
26
27
28

29

From: AnyMeeting
<noreply@anymeeting.com>
Date: Thu, Apr 18 at 6:51 PM
Subject: Please Tell Us What You Think

30
31

Alan, take AnyMeeting for a spin now!

1. Log in to your Account.
2. Click the "Start a Meeting Now" button.
3. Enter a Meeting Title, invite your attendees, and select your audio option:
   - **Discussion Mode**: Everyone can talk and be heard, or
   - **Listen-Only Mode**: Only Presenters can be heard
4. When you click "Start Meeting", the system test will automatically launch and when completed you will enter the meeting window.
   (hint - it's a rising sun!)
5. Controls are at the top of the meeting window, including "Share" to share a document, video, your entire screen or an application with your attendees.
6. Click "End Meeting" when finished.

Download our Easy Reference Guide for Presenters.

Then, start a meeting - even just to test by yourself. Log in now.

✔ Neither you nor your attendees need to download or install software from AnyMeeting, nor do attendees need an AnyMeeting account to attend.

✔ To schedule meetings for a future date - the process is the same. Then, log in just before the scheduled time, find your Upcoming Meetings and click "Start This Meeting".

✔ Here are two brief videos to help you get started:

   - Quick Start Tutorial
   - Account Manager Overview

Join us for a quickstart webinar
Our support team holds daily webinars, M-F 10am PT.

[Get Training]

Additional Resources

✔ Support website with Knowledgebase and FAQ's: support.anymeeting.com

✔ Video Tutorials covering all aspects of use: Videos

✔ Join a Live Quick Start Training Webinar: Register Now
   (available Monday to Friday at 10am Pacific with live Q&A)

As a new AnyMeeting user, you'll receive a few email lessons in the coming days, as well as an occasional newsletter and selected offers from our partners. Your email address is never sold or rented to a third party.

P.S. - Want a full-featured solution with no ads? Go Pro for as little as $17.99 a month!

 This is a great quick start guide that allows a user the feel the value of the product immediately after signup.

Lesson #1: How to Run a Meeting

Dear Alan,

Welcome again to AnyMeeting, a great tool for all your web conferencing needs. We want to ensure you hold successful meetings, so here are some basic instructions and best practices for running meetings. Watch our video tutorial, or read the instructions below.

Watch our tutorial video

How to Run a Meeting

Begin by launching a meeting from your Account Manager:

- Log in to your account
- Select "Start a Meeting Now", or "Start This Meeting" if you scheduled it in advance.
- Meeting window opens as a title slide and a rising sun.
- You'll be prompted to start your webcam (optional) and connect your audio.
- See all attendees in the left column.
- Meeting controls are along the top, including Share and Record options.
- Meeting link (url) and telephone numbers (optional) are also along the top.
  - Computer Mic and Speakers, or
  - Telephone Conference Calling (long distance charges may apply).
- Be sure to "End Meeting" at the conclusion of your session.

**Try running a meeting now --
you don't even need another participant to test it out.**

Log in to Your Account
Start a meeting now, or schedule a meeting for later.

[Log in Now]

Tips for Best Performance

Here are a few sure-fire tips to ensure that you and your attendees have the best possible online meeting.

✓ Use a wired internet connection when hosting a meeting. Wi-fi connections may result in lag or quality issues.

✓ Close all programs on your computer that you will not be using during your meeting, and open the files you will be presenting to your audience before you start the meeting.

✓ If you're using a conference call, launch the meeting and dial into the conference call 5-10 minutes before the scheduled start time. Use the mute function on your phone (*5) to eliminate background noise from the audience during your presentation.

✓ Move at a methodical pace when presenting and periodically review the audience feedback indicators.

Additional Resources

✓ Support website with Knowledgebase and FAQ's: Support

✓ Join a Live Quick Start Training Webinar: Register Now (available Monday to Friday at 10am Pacific with live Q&A

✓ Free eBook - 40 Tips for Webinar Success: Download Now

Subject:
Lesson 1 - How to Run a Meeting

Sent:
Four days after signup

Call to action:
Watch our tutorial Lon in now

While there is a lot going on in this email they use the design to break it up into readable chunks.

the anymeeting minute

MARCH 28, 2013

Hi Alan!

Happy Spring! As the weather turns warmer, now your attendees can take their iPads outside and participate in your meetings, conferences and webinars on the go! We have even more improvements planned - so stay tuned - and be sure to tell us what features are important to your small business in the survey below!

In this issue: New iPad App for Meeting Attendees + 10 tips for branding your small business.

Latest Feature Updates: AnyMeeting Releases New iPad App

Small business happens everywhere. And meetings, webinars, and video conferences must be easy to attend from anywhere. That's why we are excited to announce our new iPad app, available for download in the iTunes App Store.

Grow your Small Business

The app enables iPad users to easily attend meetings, watch screen sharing, and even broadcast their video. Now, meeting attendees participating from the iPad app, will be able to:

- View presentations.
- Listen to audio through their iPad speakers.
- Broadcast video through either the front or back camera of their iPad.

Read more...

Tips and Tricks:
10 easy marketing tips for increased brand visibility

Marketing your business can seem like a daunting task, and sometimes we just need a little guidance to set things in motion. Here are some tips that you can easily implement into your monthly routine to ensure that your brand is communicating properly with your target audience.

Follow these steps and you will be on your way to better engaging your audience and achieving greater success!

Tip # 1. Be personal and authentic in your communication – With social media at the forefront of our marketing and communications platform, it is imperative that you communicate on a personal level. People are more inclined to participate with your brand if they know there is ...

Read More

New Resources:
BYOD. Bring Your Own Device? Or Bring Your Own Disaster?

The concept of "bring your own device" (BYOD) is an unstoppable trend especially in the small business space. It's a winning combination as companies save on hardware and training costs while improving employee satisfaction.

However to embrace the power of BYOD, businesses must ensure that they have adequate protections in place to counter the associated security risks.

The first step in enhancing your small business security posture with regards to BYOD is to lay out a clear policy. It should define access methods and mandate the use of company authorized applications and security tools for employee-owned devices that access ...

Read More

Small Business Toolkit

Quality 24/7 Tech Support for Your Small Business – 33% Discount for Anymeeting Users

Anymeeting recommends 24/7 Techies for high quality tech support for your small business. For just $19.95/employee/month you get:

24/7 Techies

- 24x7 unlimited support for computers, smart devices & peripherals
- Computer & cloud application support
- Tune up and optimization services
- Help with security, email, internet issues and more

Monthly newsletter
Subject:
Newsletter: New iPad App + 10 Easy Marketing Tips for Branding Your Small Biz

Sent:
Seven days after signup

Content:
**New features
Marketing tips
Resources
Cross selling other services**

30 Days To Sell - Converting users from try to buy.

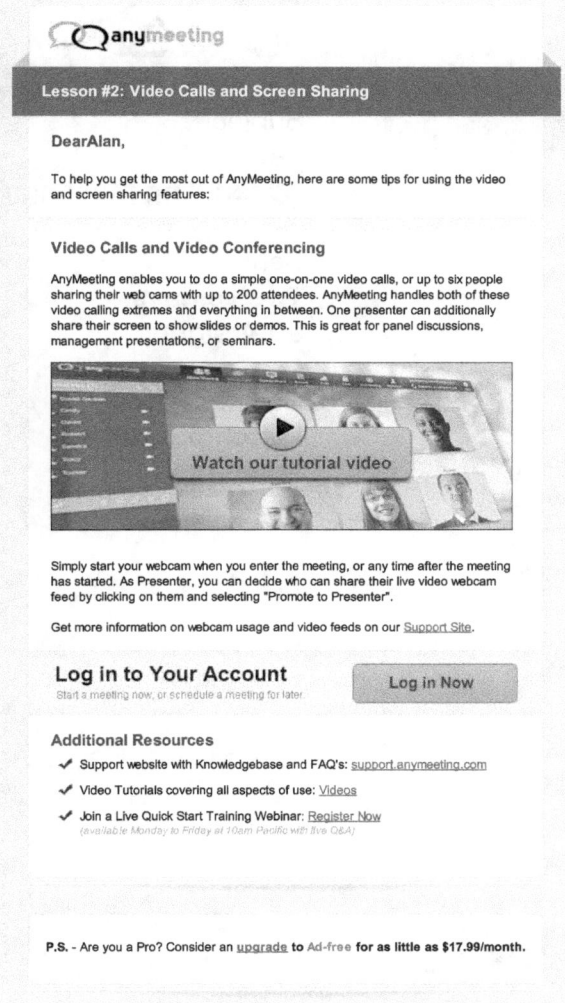

Subject:
Lesson #2: Video Calls and Screen Sharing

Sent:
Eight days after signup

Call to action:
Watch our tutorial Login now

AnyMeeting keeps the support information consistent across every email. It is helpful and reassuring for users to know support is in easy reach.

Lesson #3: Scheduling Meetings

Dear Alan,

By now, you've likely held a meeting, or two, or more... So, here's a refresher on scheduling meetings:

How to Schedule a Meeting

This 2 minute video will help make you a pro at scheduling online meetings.

To schedule a meeting for a future time, follow the wizard in your Account Manager:

- Log in to your account
- Click on the "Schedule a Meeting" button
- Enter Title, Date and Time.
- Enter emails of Attendees and any other Presenters.
  (If you don't have all e-mails handy just now, you can add and send them later.)
- Formulate your personal invitation text for the emails.
- Select Audio method:
  - Discussion Mode -- Everyone can talk and be heard
  - Listen-Only Mode -- Only Presenters can be heard
- Press "Schedule Meeting Now" to immediately send invitations to all participants, or, press "Next>>" to create a Registration Form.

Registration Forms, Surveys and Preview are advanced functions to help you make more sophisticated meeting arrangements.

You might use these optional functions to collect data from your sales prospects or to require payment to participate in your meeting or to send follow-up surveys.

Log in to Your Account

Start a meeting now, or schedule a meeting for later.

Log in Now

Some additional tips regarding invitations

As the meeting Host, you have four basic options to invite attendees:

1. **Send meeting invitations without registration.**
   This is the easiest invitation, because when you organize your meeting, every attendee will receive an e-mail with the date, time, title, personal message from you and the actual link to join the meeting. At the time of meeting, attendees simply click the meeting link, enter their name and e-mail and join the live meeting.

2. **Send meeting invitations requiring pre-registration.**
   When you schedule the meeting, click through to the Registration page and you can require additional fields and even require payment in advance for attendees. When you finish creating the meeting, invitations will be sent to all e-mail addresses announcing your meeting, which prompt recipients to click through to your registration form. Registered attendees will then receive a confirmation e-mail with actual meeting link and audio info.

3. **Public meetings promoted through Facebook and Twitter.**
   When you schedule a meeting, check the box "Make Public", and if you've connected your social accounts, then meeting notifications will be posted to those services.

Subject:
Lesson 3:
Scheduling Meetings

Sent:
Twelve days
after signup

Call to action:
Watch our tutorial
Login now

---

30 Days To Sell - Converting users from try to buy.

Lesson #4: How to Promote and Record Your Meetings

Dear Alan,

Now that you have been using AnyMeeting for a few weeks now, here are some pro tips for promoting your meetings and events:

Public Profile and Public Meetings

If you haven't already, create a Public Profile in the Account Manager. You can add your photo or company logo, link to your website, show your LinkedIn profile, Facebook Page and Twitter Feed. All your upcoming public meetings as well as past public recordings are shown. Public Profiles are discovered and indexed by search engines like Google for maximum visibility. You can distribute your own unique profile link address, too.

Next, when you Schedule a Meeting, check the box "Make Public", and your meeting will be displayed on your Profile Page and pushed out to your Facebook and Twitter feeds, if you've authorized that. You can attract more attendees and prospective customers to your meetings.

More information on Public Profiles on our Support Site

Log in to Your Account

Start a meeting now, or schedule a meeting for later

Log in Now

Recording Meetings

When you record your meetings, they will contain both audio and screen-sharing images, and they can be played back on demand. Recordings can be public or private and even have password control. You can also require registration and even charge via PayPal for users to watch your recordings. Recordings are stored on AnyMeeting's servers.

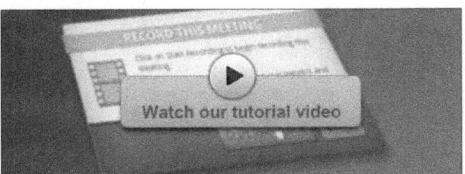

Watch our tutorial video

The basic steps to record your meeting are as follows:

- First start your meeting - when you see the rising sun, you're ready to start.
- If using Telephone conference call for audio, you must dial in now.
- Click the "Record" icon at the top of the screen.
- Run your meeting with webcams, screen sharing, etc.
- Click "Record" again to stop recording.
- Be sure to click "End Meeting" when you're finished.
- Your recording may take up to a couple hours to process.

See more recording suggestions in our Knowledge Base

Subject:
Lesson 4: How to promote and record your meetings

Sent:
Eighteen days after signup

Call to action:
**Login now
Watch our tutorial**

Please Tell Us What You Think!

Dear Alan,

By now, you've been a registered user of AnyMeeting for over a month. We hope that it has been useful to you, that you've run many meetings, and that you will continue to enjoy our many features.

We'd like to ask your help in completing a quick survey of AnyMeeting, which will be used by our development team to improve our product.

The survey will take just a few minutes of your time. You'll be asked to log in to your account if you're not already logged in.

Please click here to take our survey. We appreciate your feedback.

Take our Survey
Your feedback helps us make a better product

Take the Survey

Win a Prize!

✓ All surveys completed during each calendar month will be entered into a drawing to win a year of AnyMeeting's Ad-Free Premium Service, worth over $200!

✓ No purchase is necessary, and if you're already a paid subscriber, we'll add the prize to your current subscription.

P.S. - Have you checked out our Pro plans yet? Did you know you can upgrade to an Ad-free 200 plan for as little as $69.99/month?

AnyMeeting - 7977 Center Ave, Suite 520, Huntington Beach, CA 92647
Contact Us

Subject:
Please tell us what you think!

Sent:
Twenty nine days after signup

Call to action:
Take the survey

Edicy

Create a website for your business 30-day trial

 From: Edicy <support@edicy.com>
Date: Fri, Mar 22 at 6:48 PM
Subject: Welcome to Edicy

 01
02
03

04 **From:** Edicy <support@edicy.com>
05 **Date:** Mon, Mar 25 at 10:00 AM
Subject: Make your website work

 From: Edicy <support@edicy.com>
Date: Wed, Mar 27 at 10:01 AM
Subject: Maximize your website's
performance

06
07
08
09
10
11
12
13
14
15
16
17

18  **From:** Edicy <support@edicy.com>
19 **Date:** Mon, Apr 8 at 8:30 AM
Subject: Your Edicy subscription is about
20 to expire
21
22
23
24

From: Edicy <support@edicy.com>
Date: Mon, Apr 15 at 9:08 AM
Subject: Your Edicy subscription is about
to expire

25
26
27
28
29
30
31

30 Days To Sell - Converting users from try to buy.

edicy   GO TO EDICY.COM   GET SUPPORT   LOG IN TO YOUR SITE

Get started with your **website.**

Hi there!

Thanks for signing up for a 30 day Edicy Plus trial and creating your fresh beautifulben.edicy.co site. To get started, log in from Edicy website with alanresearch36@gmail.com address and selected password.

Next step:

Learn how to launch your site.

Talk soon,
The people at Edicy

Subject:
Welcome to Edicy!

Sent:
Immediately

Call to action:
Login to start
Learn how to launch
your site

---

edicy   GO TO EDICY.COM   GET SUPPORT   LOG IN TO YOUR SITE

Make your website work.

Hi again!

You've recently started building your beautifulben.edicy.co website with Edicy. Let us help you with a few quick tips.

- How to choose a design theme.
- How to edit images online with Edicy.
- What does each Edicy menu button do?

Talk soon,
The people at Edicy

Subject:
Make your
website work

Sent:
Three days
after signup

Call to action:
Choose a design

edicy   GO TO EDICY.COM   GET SUPPORT   LOG IN TO YOUR SITE

Maximize your website's performance.

Hi again!

Your beautifulben.edicy.co website is getting better. We wanted to suggest you a few other tips that help you maximize the performance of your website.

- How to add widgets
- How to set up Google Analytics account
- How to set up a form for online orders, contacting etc.
- How to create a successful company blog

Please let us know if we can be of more help for you in any way.

Thanks,
The people at Edicy

Subject:
Maximize your website's performance

Sent:
Five days after signup

Call to action:
Add more features

---

edicy   GO TO EDICY.COM   GET SUPPORT   LOG IN TO YOUR SITE

Your Edicy subscription is about to **expire.**

Hi there!

Your Edicy Plus trial for the website at beautifulben.edicy.co is going to expire in 13 days, on **April 21, 2013**. To continue using Edicy, you'll need to purchase a subscription (€14/mo or €120/yr) in the Account section under Settings menu.

Buy the subscription

All the best!
The people at Edicy

Subject:
Your Edicy subscription is about to expire

Sent:
Seventeen days after signup

Call to action:
Buy the subscription

edicy   GO TO EDICY.COM   GET SUPPORT   LOG IN TO YOUR SITE

Your Edicy subscription is about to **expire.**

Hi there!

Your Edicy Plus trial for the website at beautifulben.edicy.co is going to expire in 13 days, on **April 21, 2013**. To continue using Edicy, you'll need to purchase a subscription (€14/mo or €120/yr) in the Account section under Settings menu.

Buy the subscription

All the best!
The people at Edicy

Subject:
Your Edicy subscription is about to expire

Sent:
Twenty four days after signup

Call to action:
Buy the subscription

Please do not respond

The door to door salesman asks how you are and before you can answer "well actually I have a pot over boiling on the stove, please hang on just a moment..." he launches into his sales speech. You are too polite to just close the door on him but man are you annoyed. You can't wait untill you get to tell him a flat "no" at the end of his spiel. That's how it feels to get email marketing from do-not-reply@yourcompany.com.

There are many reasons to use an email address like do-not-reply@ yourcompany.com, but frankly none of them are good enough. The most common reason companies give is that there is no one to receive and answer any replies and automated out of office email. I suggest it is time to make someone available.

Here is an opportunity to use one of the greatest strengths of email marketing in the sales process. The personal touch.

No one wants to deal with a big faceless corporation or automated machine. They want the confidence and reassurance that if they have any problems, even if they never will, there is someone who can help them. It is one of the reasons landing pages with a phone number convert so much better than those without. Though very few people will ever call that number, the fact it exists reassures many prospective buyers to go ahead and purchase in confidence.

As you noticed in the welcome mails on page 06, the personal touch, a name and face for your dedicated account manager, works really well.

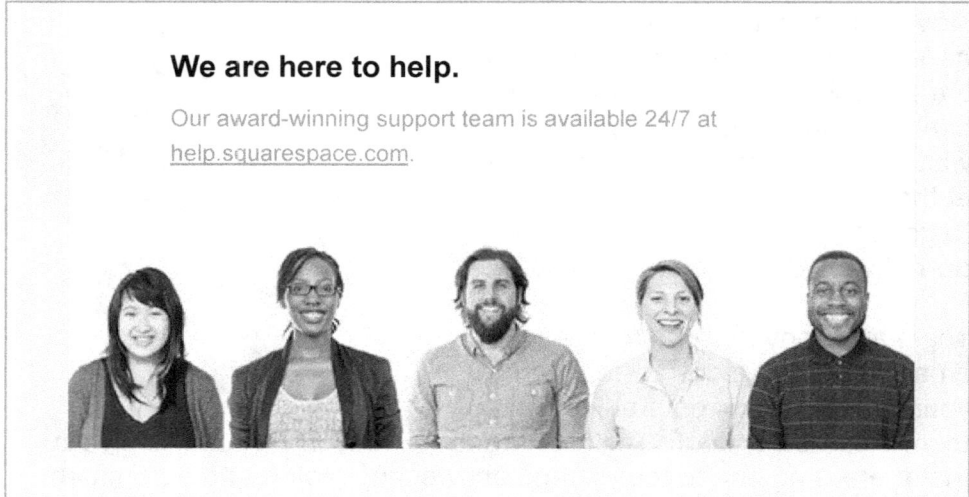

But it is very easy to undermine this with a do-not-reply email address. If I reply to Alex, my personal account manager in my Shopify welcome email and I am presented with do-not-reply, I am going to feel pretty cheated. If I am going to spend money with you, I want to feel I will be listened to.

But beyond the sales or social impact of telling a prospect you do not want to listen to them there are a few technical aspects as well. Some people try to unsubscribe from emails by hitting reply and asking to be removed. It can be annoying for you, sure, but its a whole lot better than their next step.

If they can't reply their next action will be to hit the 'this is spam' button in their email client.

When you get many spam reports you will end up having dificulty delivering any emails at all. Your time and investment is lost.

To ensure emails get delivered in future many companies emails ask a reader to add the email address to their contacts list. No one is going to add do-not-reply@yourcompany.com to their contacts list.

Some countries, especially in Europe, have a legal requirement that you must be able to reply to an email. Do-not-reply could mean you are breaking the law.

Finally, there is a slightly sneaky reason to accept replies from your email marketing. Out of office replies. When you email a prospect and get an out of office reply you are usually presented with a wealth of information you may not have had on the prospect. Name, job title, department and other information is often contained. This can help you segment future emails to this and other prospects. Also if the person leaves the company you get notified so you can remove them from your list before your emails start getting automatically marked as spam.

```
Out of office: Welcome to Acme inc
```

```
From Stewart
To: do-no-reply@acmeinc.com

I am currently out of the office at a job interview
and will reply to you if I fail to get the position.
Please be prepared for my mood.

Regards, Stewart.
```

Back to the door-to-door salesman who has no interest in listening to anything you have to say. It's rude. And no one wants to buy from a rude person.

Genbook

Online scheduling software 30-day trial

 From: Genbook <no_reply@genbook.com>
Date: Fri, Mar 22 at 6:52 PM
Subject: Welcome to Genbook!

01

 From: Genbook <no_reply@genbook.com>
Date: Fri, Mar 22 at 6:52 PM
Subject: Genbook - Confirm your email
address

02

 From: Cornelia Waters - Genbook Support
<support@genbook.com>
Date: Sun, Mar 24 at 1:19 AM
Subject: Need help with Genbook?

03

04

05

06

 From: Genbook <no_reply@genbook.com>
Date: Wed, Mar 27 at 7:17 PM
Subject: Need some help with Genbook?

07

08

09

10

11

12

13

14

15

16

17

18

19

20

21

22

 From: Genbook <no_reply@genbook.com>
Date: Sat, Apr 13 at 2:04 AM
Subject: Your free trial ends in 7 days

23

24

25

26

27

28

 From: Genbook <no_reply@genbook.com>
Date: Thu, Apr 18 at 2:21 AM
Subject: Your free trial ends very soon

29

30

 From: Genbook <no_reply@genbook.com>
Date: Sat, Apr 20 at 2:12 AM
Subject: Your free trial has ended

31

30 Days To Sell - Converting users from try to buy.

Genbook

Hello Beautiful ben,

Welcome to Genbook and thanks for signing up! Your 30-Day Free Trial has now started.

Please complete your account setup soon so your customers can begin scheduling their appointments online.

> Login to Genbook

Have questions? We have answers. You now have full access to our super-smart and super-friendly Customer Care Team. Just send us a message from within your Genbook Account, and we will respond promptly.

Thank you,
The Customer Care Team

Subject:
Welcome to Genbook!

Sent:
Immediately

Call to action:
Login to Genbook

Genbook

Hello alanresearch36@gmail.com,

Please click the button below to confirm your e-mail address.

> Validate my email address

Or copy and paste this link into your web browser:

http://www.genbook.com/manager/user/605061058/validate?email=alanresearch36%40gmail.com&hash=V%2FnW8aYhyrOabAFbQEeXU9yQRC8%3D

Thank you,
The Customer Care Team

Subject:
Genbook - Confirm your email address

Sent:
Immediately

Call to action:
Validate my email address

Subject:
Need some help with Genbook?

Sent:
Two days after signup

Call to action:
Reply if you have any questions

Subject:
Need some help with Genbook?

Sent:
Five days after signup

Call to action:
Do you need any help setting up your account?

30 Days To Sell - Converting users from try to buy.

Genbook

Hello Beautiful ben,

We hope that you and your customers are enjoying your free trial of Genbook, which ends in 7 days.

To ensure there is no interruption to your service, please login to your account, choose a plan, and submit valid credit card details. If payment information is not received within 7 days, you will lose access to your Genbook account. Your prompt action is appreciated.

Login to Genbook

Have questions? We have answers. You now have full access to our super-smart and super-friendly Customer Care Team. Just send us a message from within your Genbook Account, and we will respond promptly.

Thank you,
The Customer Care Team

Subject:
Your free trial ends in 7 days

Sent:
Twenty two days after signup

Call to action:
Login to Genbook

Genbook

Hello Beautiful ben,

Your free trial will end on Apr 20. If your payment information is not received by then, you will lose access to your Genbook account and your customers won't be able to schedule online.

Please login to your account immediately and submit valid credit card details in order to continue using Genbook.

Login to Genbook

If you have any questions, please contact the Customer Care Team from within your Genbook Account.

Thank you,
The Customer Care Team

Subject:
Your free trial ends very soon

Sent:
Twenty seven days after signup

Call to action:
Login to Genbook

Genbook

Hello Beautiful ben,

Your 30-day free trial of Genbook has now ended!

But don't worry - we have saved your configuration and you can easily re-open your account. To resume your service, please login to your account and submit valid credit card details.

Login to Genbook

If you have any questions, please contact the Customer Care Team from within your Genbook Account.

Thank you,
The Customer Care Team

Subject:
Your free trial has ended

Sent:
Twenty nine days after signup

Call to action:
Login to Genbook

30 Days To Sell - Converting users from try to buy.

Mailgun

Programmable mail servers 30-day trial

 From: Mailgun Support
<support@mailgun.net>
Date: Thu, Mar 28 at 5:31 PM
Subject: Welcome to Mailgun!

 From: Mailgun <michael@mailgunhq.com>
Date: Fri, Mar 29 at 5:31 PM
Subject: Getting started with Mailgun

03

04

05

06

07

 From: Mailgun <michael@mailgunhq.com>
Date: Fri, Apr 5 at 5:31 PM
Subject: Mucho Mailgun code samples
and documentation

09

10

11

12

13

14

 **From:** Mailgun <michael@mailgunhq.com>
Date: Fri, Apr 12 at 6:31 PM
Subject: More Mailgun code samples

16

17

18

19

20

21

 From: Mailgun <michael@mailgunhq.com>
Date: Fri, Apr 19 at 6:31 PM
Subject: Try Mailgun Standard
plan for free. It's legit.

22

23

24

25

26

27 **Monthly newsletter**
From: Mailgun <michael@mailgunhq.com>
Date: Wed, Apr 24 at 9:04 PM
Subject: Better webhooks, geolocation and
more in this month's newsletter

28

29

30

31

30 Days To Sell - Converting users from try to buy.

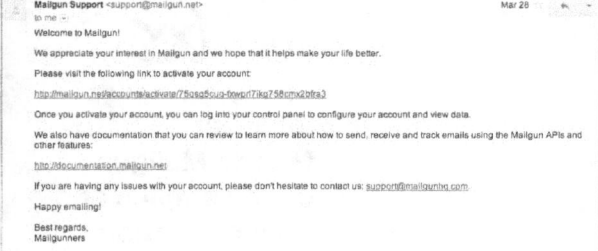

01

Subject:
Welcome to Mailgun!

Sent:
Immediately

Call to action:
Activate your account

02

Subject:
Getting started with Mailgun

Sent:
Next day after signup

Call to action:
Any questions about getting started?

30 Days To Sell - Converting users from try to buy.

08

Subject:
Mucho Mailgun code samples and documentation

Sent:
Seven days after signup

Call to action:
Check our documentation

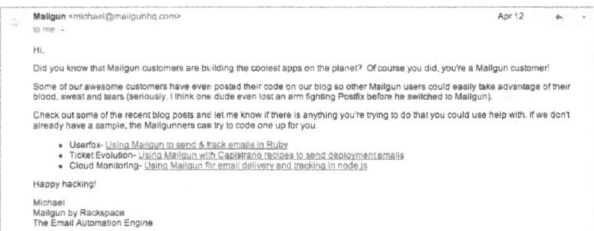

15

Subject:
More Mailgun code samples

Sent:
Fourteen days after signup

Call to action:
Other people that use Mailgun

Mailgun <michael@mailgunhq.com> Apr 19
to me

Hi,

It's Michael from Mailgun again. We have a lot of customers who use the Mailgun Quick Setup option because it's, well, quick. The downside is that all your emails appear to come from *yourdomain.mailgun.org* instead of simply *yourdomain.com*. That's kind of like starting your own business and using your gmail address to email with clients. Pretty weak.

Mailgun makes it really easy to send emails from your own domain. You can always contact us using live chat on our website if you need help but here are the basic steps:

- Upgrade your account from free plan to the standard plan. **Use the coupon *tryfree* in the next 14 days and receive a $19/discount on your first bill.** That's enough to send up to 19,000 emails completely for free.
- Add your domain in the Domains tab of the Mailgun Control Panel
- Set up SPF, DKIM and CNAME records following the instructions in the Control Panel
- Fist pump because that's it. No more mailgun.org in your emails.

Happy hacking!

Michael
Mailgun by Rackspace
The Email Automation Engine

Subject:
**Try Mailgun
Standard plan for
free. It's legit.**

Sent:
**Twenty one days
after signup**

Call to action:
**Upgrade your
account**

  April, 2013

Domain-level webhooks are here

You've asked for domain-level webhooks and now they're here. With this new feature, each domain in your account can have its own webhook endpoint. This is especially helpful if you are managing email for your own clients and want to segregate webhooks or if you have separate staging and production environments.

Domain-level webhooks

Build more sophisticated reports using custom variables

Mailgun customers are building some pretty sophisticated apps that rely on tracking each individual email. Now you can add unlimited custom variables into email headers, making it easier to match each email back to the advanced segments you want to track.

Custom variables how-to

Geolocation and user-agent parameters now available in webhooks

Customers have been asking for IP address and user-agent string to be passed with webhook data. Well ask no more. In addition to the raw IP and user-agent string, Mailgun will pass over Country, Region, City, Device, Operation System and Client.

Geolocation

Weekly product updates

We try to be as agile as possible with Mailgun, rolling out small new features regularly, versus large improvements once a blue moon. We've starting publishing weekly product updates to keep you informed of what is going on with Mailgun so you can keep integrating the newest features into your app.

Weekly updates

We've got a new blog

If you haven't noticed yet, we completely revamped our blog to make it easier to read and discover related posts and documentation that will help you do more with Mailgun. Code samples look great, screen shots are bigger and you can subscribe to stay up-to-date with the latest Mailgun news. We hope you enjoy it.

New blog

Customer case studies

Build a Meteor-Mailgun app in less than 5 minutes »
Curious about the new JS-based web framework Meteor? Check out how to build an email-enabled web app on Meteor in less than 5 minutes. Read the blog »

Building a better project management app with Mailgun »
Learn how Kanban2Go built a better project management app by letting their users create new tasks simply by sending an email. Read the blog »

Monthly newsletter

Subject:
Better webhooks, geolocation and more in this month's newsletter

Sent:
Twenty six days after signup

Content:
New features
How-to guides
New blog

Cazoomi

Data syncing 15-day trial

 From: Cazoomi SyncApps
<syncapps@cazoomi.com>
Date: Thu, May 2 at 12:58 PM
Subject: Please verify your registration

 01

02

03

04

05

06

07

08 **From:** Clint Wilson <clint@cazoomi.com>
Date: Thu, May 9 at 1:10 PM
Subject: Cazoomi SyncApps trial account

09

10

11

12

13

14

 From: Cazoomi SyncApps
<syncapps@cazocmi.com>
Date: Thu, May 16 at 12:10 PM
Subject: Your Cazoomi SyncApps trial has ended

15

16

17

18

19

20

21

22

23

24

25

26

27

28

29

30

31

30 Days To Sell - Converting users from try to buy.

SyncApps®
by CAZOOMI

Hi Alan,

Thank you for registering on syncapps.cazoomi.com.

Click the link below to verify your email address and activate your account:
https://syncapps.cazoomi.com/application/activateaccount?emailAddress=alanresearch38%40gmail.com&key=GFnWg11i

Once your account is activated you will have access to SyncApps. If you did not register for Cazoomi SyncApps please disregard this email.

Regards,
Cazoomi Teams
415.400.4541

Subject:
Please verify your registration

Sent:
Immediately

Call to action:
Verify your email

SyncApps®
by CAZOOMI

Hi Alan,

I just wanted to check in to see how it's going with your SyncApps trial.

We want you to know that we're on hand to help you with any questions or issues that come up as you're getting the software up and running for your company. We want your experience to be the best that it can be, so if you need any help at all don't hesitate to ask.

Here are three easy ways to get support, buy SyncApps and email:

- Go to http://community.cazoomi.com
- Buy SyncApps: https://syncapps.cazoomi.com/upgrade
- E-mail ask@cazoomi.com

Thanks again for trying SyncApps by Cazoomi.

Clint Wilson
Director, Customer Experience

clint@cazoomi.com
t: 415.400.4541
www.cazoomi.com

Subject:
Cazoomi SyncApps trial account

Sent:
Seven days after signup

Call to action:
Get support

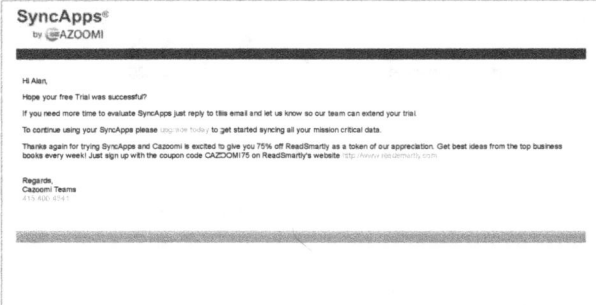

Subject:
**Your Cazoomi
SyncApps trial has
ended**

Sent:
**Eight days after
signup**

Call to action:
Upgrade today

Microsoft 365
Office communication & collaboration services

 From: Microsoft Office <reply@email.office.com>
Date: 14 November 22:36
Subject: What's new in Office? Open and see.

01

02 **From:** Microsoft Office <reply@email.office.com>
Date: 15 November 16:33
Subject: Your Office, your way. Just sign in.

03

04

05

 From: Microsoft Office <reply@email.office.com>
Date: 19 November 16:34
Subject: Save, access and edit with Office in the cloud.

06

07

08

09

10

11 **From:** Microsoft Office <reply@email.office.com>
Date: 24 November 16:38
Subject: Invite your coworkers. Add users to Office Preview.

12

13

14

15

16

17

 From: Take an interactive tour of the Office applications.
Date: 1 December 16:39
Subject: Take an interactive tour of the Office applications.

18

19

20

21

22

23

24

25 **From:** Microsoft Office 365 Team <MicrosoftOffice365@email.office.com>
Date: 8 December 16:42
Subject: See what's new in the Office applications.

26

27

28

29

 From: Microsoft Office 365 Team <MicrosoftOffice365@email.office.com>
Date: 15 December 16:43
Subject: Use Office 365 to work together in the cloud.

30

31

 1

30 Days To Sell - Converting users from try to buy.

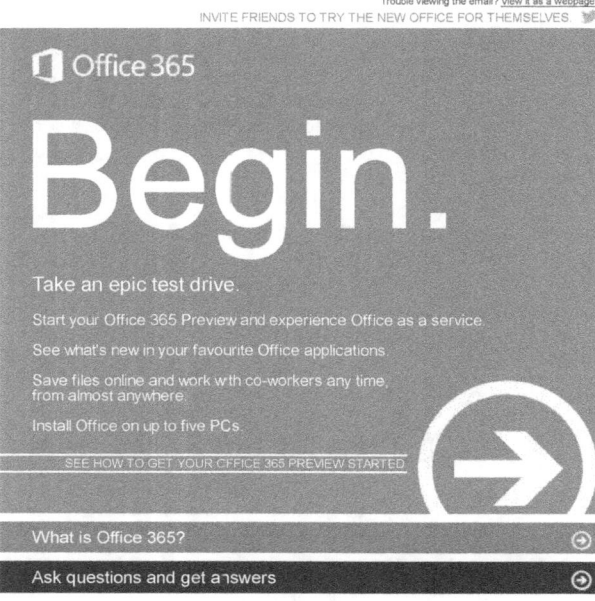

Office 365

Begin.

Take an epic test drive.

Start your Office 365 Preview and experience Office as a service.

See what's new in your favourite Office applications.

Save files online and work with co-workers any time, from almost anywhere.

Install Office on up to five PCs.

SEE HOW TO GET YOUR OFFICE 365 PREVIEW STARTED

What is Office 365?

Ask questions and get answers

BECOME A FACEBOOK FAN AND FOLLOW US ON TWITTER TO GET THE LATEST INFO ON OFFICE.

Terms of Use   Trademarks   Privacy Statement   Unsubscribe   *Microsoft*

Subject:
**What's new in Office?
Open and see.**

Sent:
Immediately

Call to action:
**See how to get
started**

This sequence of emails for the launch of Microsoft Office 365 is more of a teaser than an activation campaign but it is a great example of explaining the features and benefits of a product. For an activation campaign you need a stronger call to action.

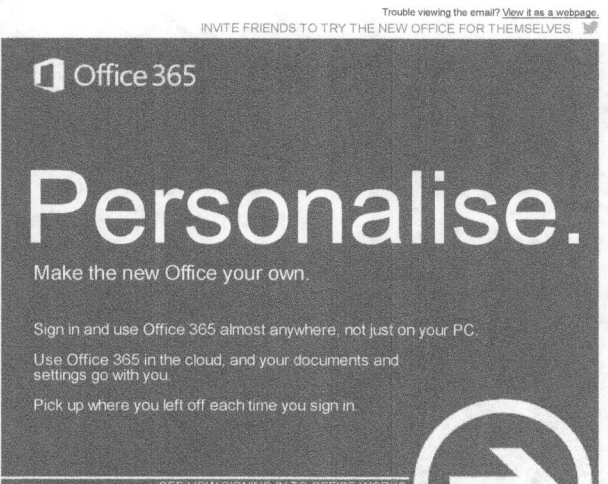

Trouble viewing the email? View it as a webpage.
INVITE FRIENDS TO TRY THE NEW OFFICE FOR THEMSELVES.

Office 365

Personalise.

Make the new Office your own.

Sign in and use Office 365 almost anywhere, not just on your PC.

Use Office 365 in the cloud, and your documents and settings go with you.

Pick up where you left off each time you sign in.

SEE HOW SIGNING IN TO OFFICE WORKS

BECOME A FACEBOOK FAN AND FOLLOW US ON TWITTER TO GET THE LATEST INFO ON OFFICE.

Microsoft Office
One Microsoft Way,
Redmond, WA.
98052 USA

Copyright 2012 Microsoft Corporation Terms of Use | Trademarks | Privacy Statement | Unsubscribe **Microsoft**

02

Subject:
**Your Office, your way.
Just sign in.**

Sent:
One day after signup

Call to action:
Signin

INVITE FRIENDS TO TRY THE NEW OFFICE FOR THEMSELVES.

BECOME A FACEBOOK FAN AND FOLLOW US ON TWITTER TO GET THE LATEST INFO ON OFFICE.

Subject:
Save, access and edit with Office in the cloud.

Sent:
Five days after signup

Call to action:
See how to save to the cloud

Office 365

Multiply.

Transform one nerve center into many.

Add users in your organization.

Discover how the new Office makes it easy to work with others.

Stay in sync and collaborate effortlessly with colleagues and customers.

SEE HOW TO ADD ANOTHER USER TO OFFICE PREVIEW

BECOME A FACEBOOK FAN AND FOLLOW US ON TWITTER TO GET THE LATEST INFO ON OFFICE.

Microsoft Office
One Microsoft Way
Redmond, WA
98052 USA

Subject:
Invite your coworkers. Add users to Office Preview.

Sent:
Ten days after signup

Call to action:
See how to add users

Office 365

Develop.

Use trusted tools in brilliant new ways.

Open an interactive tour directly from a document in Preview.

Explore the next generation of Word, Excel, PowerPoint, and Publisher.

Discover some of our favourite new features.

SEE HOW TO START AN INTERACTIVE TOUR

BECOME A FACEBOOK FAN AND FOLLOW US ON TWITTER TO GET THE LATEST INFO ON OFFICE.

Terms of Use | Trademarks | Privacy Statement | Unsubscribe   **Microsoft**

Subject:
Take an interactive tour of the Office applications.

Sent:
Seventeen days after signup

Call to action:
Start an interactive tour

Trouble viewing the email? View it as a webpage.
INVITE FRIENDS TO TRY THE NEW OFFICE FOR THEMSELVES.

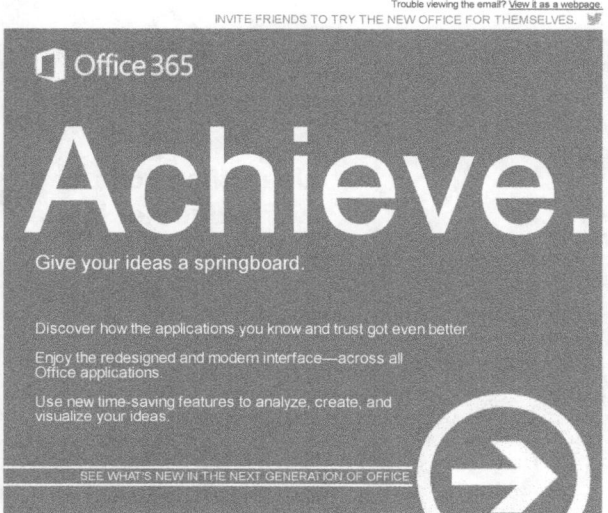

Office 365

Achieve.

Give your ideas a springboard.

Discover how the applications you know and trust got even better.

Enjoy the redesigned and modern interface—across all Office applications.

Use new time-saving features to analyze, create, and visualize your ideas.

SEE WHAT'S NEW IN THE NEXT GENERATION OF OFFICE

BECOME A FACEBOOK FAN AND FOLLOW US ON TWITTER TO GET THE LATEST INFO ON OFFICE.

Microsoft Office
One Microsoft Way
Redmond, WA
98052 USA

Copyright 2012 Microsoft Corporation Terms of Use | Trademarks | Privacy Statement | Unsubscribe   *Microsoft*

Subject:
See what's new in the Office applications.

Sent:
Twenty four days after signup

Call to action:
See whats new

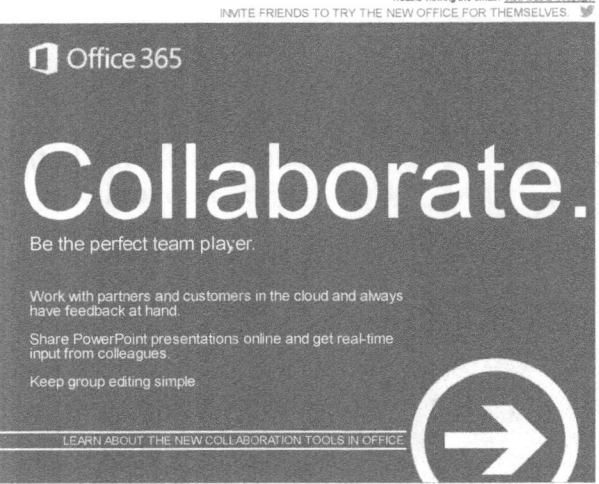

Subject:
Use Office 365 to work together in the cloud.

Sent:
31 days after signup

Call to action:
Learn about the new collaboration tools

30 Days To Sell - Converting users from try to buy.

Behaviour triggered emails

Imagine a world where you did not have to guess the sequence of emails to send out when a user signs up. Where you did not have to test the best times to send by random trial and error. And where you did not have to read a user's mind to figure out what they might want to know right now. Or even better, imagine knowing a user is in front of their computer right now, ready to use your software and all you need to do is tell them what step to take next. Welcome to behaviour triggered email.

The concept is simple. Look at what a user does, or does not do, on your website and send them the right email accordingly.

Bug tracking and support software BugHerd keeps a user in a sequence of emails to get them to install a piece of software on the users website. Only when that action is complete will Bugherd move the user into a different sequence of emails showing how to use the system.
Or, if the user does not install the piece of code, Bugherd can move the user into a retention sequence to get the user interested in the software again or find out why the user lost interest.

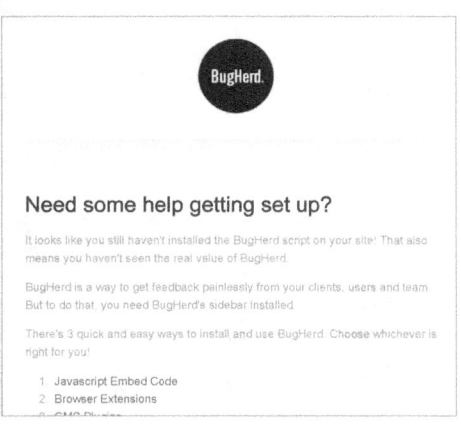

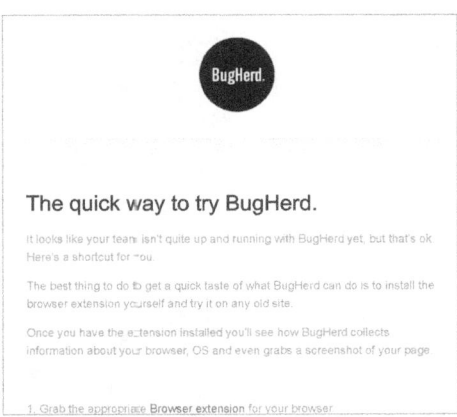

This approach allows you to focus on your core activation metric. Instead of a series of 5 emails over 30 days highlighting different aspects of your service you can run a series of mails pushing a single step without which the user cannot progress in your product. When, and only when the user carries out the action do you resume the broader sequence.

Blogging platform Tumblr.com monitors what a user has done and what they have yet to do. Crossing out or ticking the action a user has already done reinforces the required user behavour and gives a sense of completion that people respond very well to. Tumbler does not bombard a user with the full list, but just the next required action. The next action is also being triggered directly from the email making the step seem even easier.

Welcome to Tumblr!

Tumblr is the best place to find and share the coolest stuff in the world.

1. Upload a blog portrait.

Looking good.

2. Choose a design for your blog.

Ashley

A Readable & Responsive Theme for Tumblr

I'm Sick of Your Tiny, Tiny Ty

Your tiny type is hard to read - no, not hard to read, impossible to read with me everywhere, but I always seem to forget my magnifying glass. Reader button, but that's not a solution to the problem. That's a band-a typesetting.

Ashley by jxnblk

THE
SMARTEST THING
SHE'S EVER
SAID

ANN TAYLOR

Art She Said by alldayeveryday

Vacant

Vacant by samstefan

CM TUMBLR THEME

CLUB MONACO LOOKBOOK PAGE

Club Monaco Theme by clubmonaco

And thousands more!

Visit the Theme Garden

tumblr.

35 East 21st St. 10th Floor. New York, NY 10010.
Email settings | Opt-out

Many e-commerce sites ask a user at the start of the process to tell them their preferences. The retailer can then customise the emails to follow to what is most likely to turn that user into a customer.

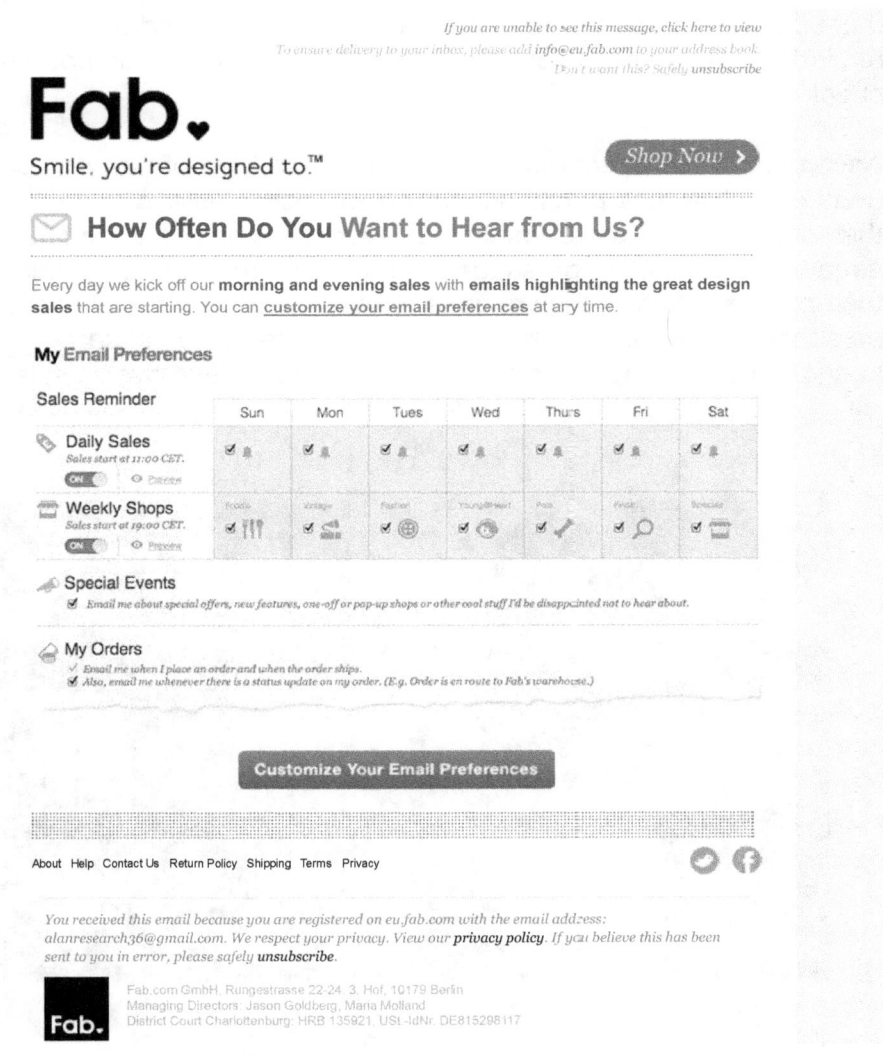

Monitoring a users behaviour does not just apply to the sign up process. Automatically tracking user actions and triggering emails has increased revenue for many e-commerce sites by up to 30%. At the end of the sales funnel this is called shopping cart abandonment. Wallmart.

com will watch for when you are looking at buying an android tablet for example. If you look at a particular model on their website, or go so far as adding it to your shopping basket but then walk away before finishing the purchase. An email will automatically be triggered to you. It could have a special offer for the item you just viewed or just a simple reminder that you have items in your shopping cart and do not forget to check out.

According to the Direct Marketing Association 65% of new customers don't complete their purchases online, choosing instead to abandon their carts. 90% of these lost leads never come back and you have a matter of minutes to persuade them to turn around and complete their purchase before they're gone forever. Sending perfectly timed, personalised messages achieves up to 20% reduction in cart abandonment and result in a 15% to 30% increase in overall sales.

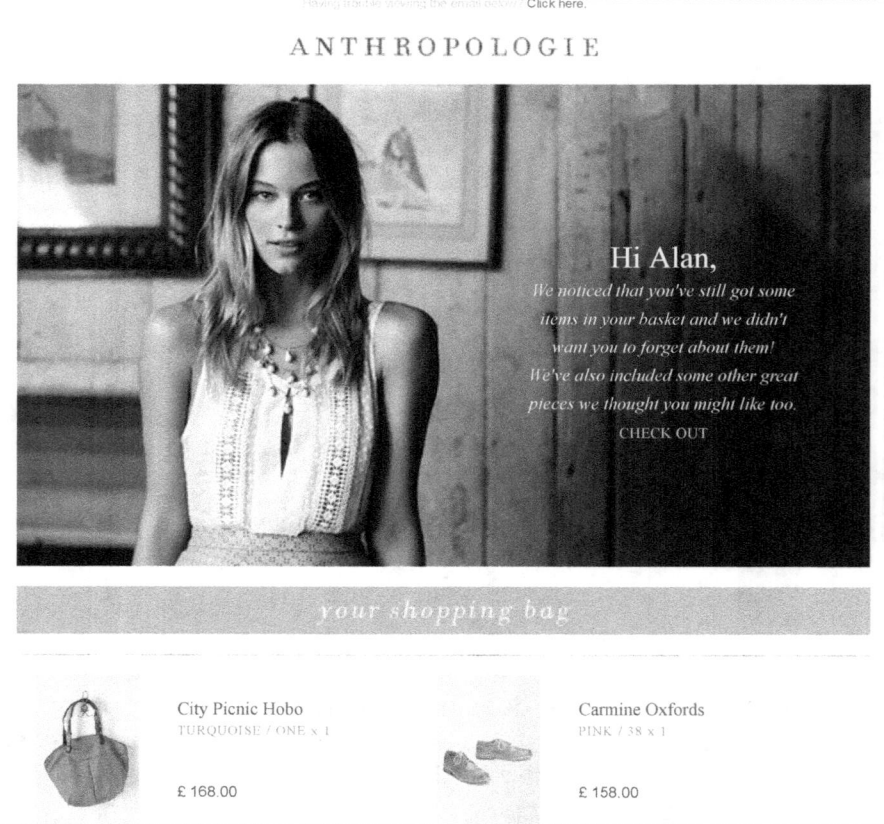

MADE

Hi Alan,

We saved these for you:

	Kick-Ass 2 Bean Bag, Action Cover	£99.00	1	£99.00

Don't worry, you won't need to go back through the site to find what you fancied. We've kept it for you here.

We can't promise they'll stay in stock though. So if you're still keen, don't leave it too long.

Why Shop With Made.Com?

We cut out the middlemen and go direct to the makers. It means we can offer our customers up to 70% off the high street, but as our products are made to order they may take a little longer getting to you. We promise they're worth the wait though.

+ 100% secure transactions
+ Fuss-free returns

Got any questions? We're here to help. Just hit reply and ask away.

To see if your items are still available and check out...   RETURN TO BASKET

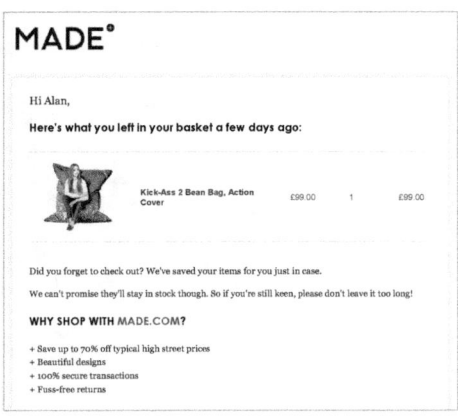

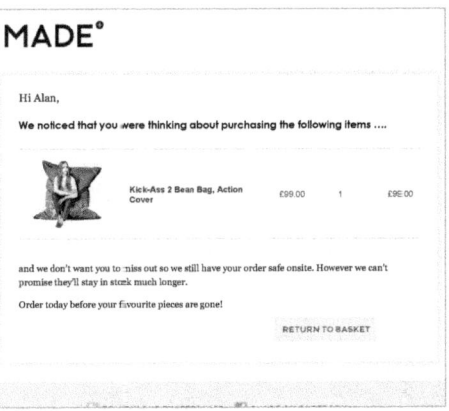

Fab
Online e-commerce store

Fab.

From: Fab <info@eu.fab.com>
Date: Wed, Jun 19 at 4:43 PM
Subject: Congrats! Your Account is Created

01

02

From: Fab <info@eu.fab.com>
Date: Wed, Jun 19 at 4:43 PM
Subject: Please confirm your email address

03

04

From: Fab <reminder@eu.fab.com>
Date: Fri, Jun 21 at 6:18 PM
Subject: Customize Your Fab Email
Preferences

From: Fab <reminder@eu.fab.com>
Date: Sun, Jun 23 at 6:26 PM
Subject: Shop With Your Friends on Fab!

05

06

07

08

From: Fab <reminder@eu.fab.com>
Date: Tue, Jun 25 at 6:34 PM
Subject: Get The Fab Mobile App!

09

From: Fab <info@eu.fab.com>
Date: Thu, Jun 27 at 1:00 PM
Subject: Free Shipping On Your First
Order. 48 Hours Only. Discover Your Design
Inspiration Today.

10

11

12

13

14

15

16

17

18

Daily Newsletters
From: Fab <reminder@eu.fab.com>
Date: 2-4 daily (depending on preferences)
Subject: Latest [category] products

19

20

21

22

23

24

25

26

27

28

29

30

31

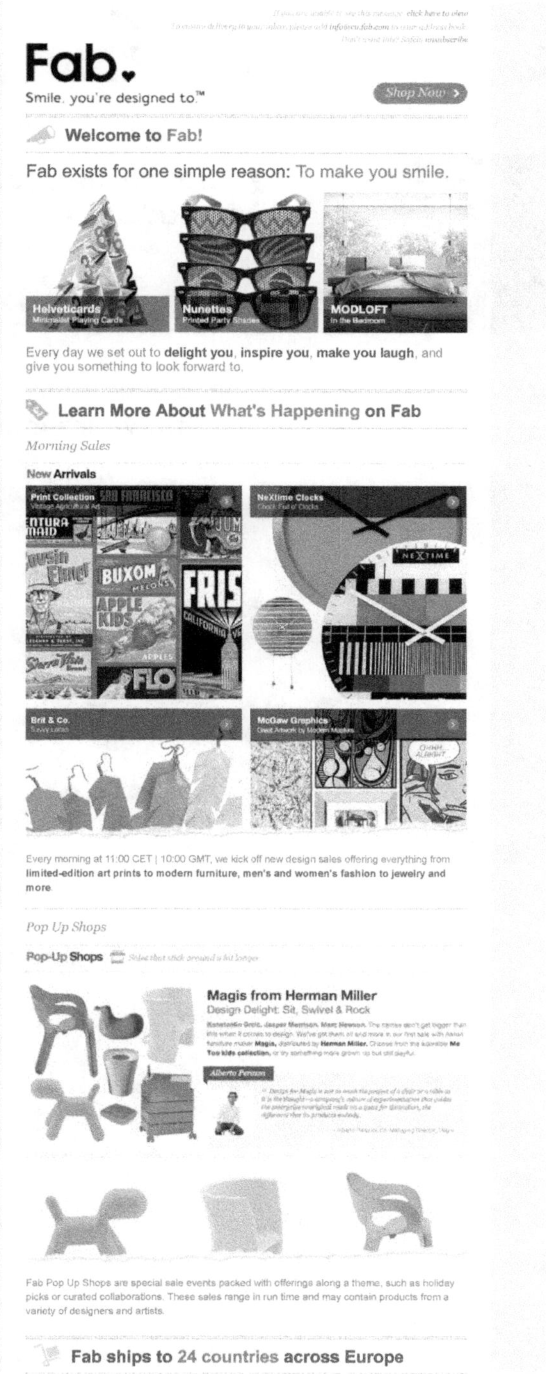

Fab.

Smile. you're designed to.™

Shop Now >

🎉 **Welcome to** Fab!

Fab exists for one simple reason: To make you smile.

Helveticards Minimalist Playing Cards

Nunettes Printed Party Shades

MODLOFT In the Bedroom

Every day we set out to **delight you**, **inspire you**, **make you laugh**, and give you something to look forward to.

🏷️ **Learn More About** What's Happening on Fab

Morning Sales

New Arrivals

Print Collection Vintage Agricultural Art

NeXtime Clocks Check Fast o' Clocks

Brit & Co. Savvy cards

McGaw Graphics Great Artwork by Modern Masters

Every morning at 11:00 CET | 10:00 GMT, we kick off new design sales offering everything from **limited-edition art prints to modern furniture, men's and women's fashion to jewelry and more**.

Pop Up Shops

Pop-Up Shops

Magis from Herman Miller Design Delight: Sit, Swivel & Rock

Alberto Perazza

Fab Pop Up Shops are special sale events packed with offerings along a theme, such as holiday picks or curated collaborations. These sales range in run time and may contain products from a variety of designers and artists.

🛒 **Fab ships to** 24 countries **across Europe**

Subject:
Congrats! Your Account is Created

Sent:
Immediately

Call to action:
Shop now

30 Days To Sell - Converting users from try to buy.

Fab.

Smile, you're designec to.®

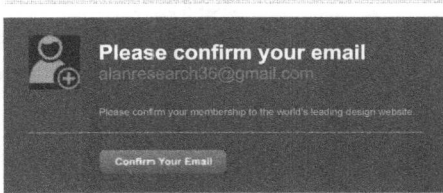

Please confirm your email

alanresearch36@gmail.com

Please confirm your membership to the world's leading design website.

Confirm Your Email

About   Help   Contact Us   Return Policy   Shipping   Terms   Privacy

You received this email because you are registered on en.fab.com with the email address: alanresearchph@gmail.com. We respect your privacy. View our *privacy policy*. If you believe this has been sent to you in error, please safely *unsubscribe*.

Fab.com GmbH, Turmstrasse 22/24, 2, Hof, 10559 Berlin.
Managing Directors: Jason Goldberg, Merle Magson
District Court Charlottenburg, HRB 135525, VAT no: DE290910

01

Subject:
Please confirm your email address

Sent:
Immediately

Call to action:
Confirm your email

Subject:
Customize Your Fab Email Preferences

Sent:
2 days after signup

Call to action:
Shop now

Customize your email preferences

30 Days To Sell - Converting users from try to buy.

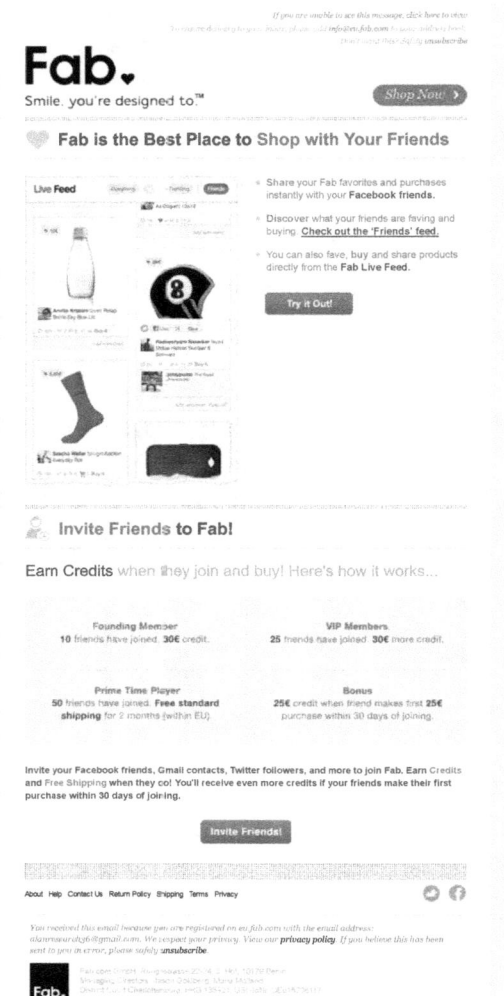

Subject:
Shop With Your Friends on Fab!

Sent:
4 days after signup

Call to action:
Shop now

Try it out

Invite friends

Subject:
Get The Fab Mobile App!

Sent:
6 days after signup

Call to action:
Shop now

Get the Fab mobile app

Subject:
**Free Shipping On
Your First Order.
48 Hours Only.
Discover Your Design
Inspiration Today.**

Sent:
8 days after signup

Call to action:
Shop now

Fab.

Smile. you're designed to.®

Shop Now ❯

If you are unable to see this message, click here to view

🎵 Vintage **Monday**

🕒 *Sales start today at 19:00 CET | 18:00 GMT*

Vintage isn't out-dated—it's the key to updating. This week, we've chosen vintage accents to instantly refresh your home or **transform your outfit.** Choose from **Birkin,** and **Kelly bags by Hermès,** chic antique **lighting and storage, anatomical prints** from the past, recycled and up-cycled **home décor** and lots more.

The Home Of Vintage Hermès

Enamel Shades

Vyconic

Little Pop Machine

Curious Prints

Randle And Eighth

📱 **Download the Fab App for your** iPhone, iPad and Android.

About Help Contact Us Return Policy Shipping Terms Privacy   🐦 📘

*You received this email because you are registered on eu.fab.com with the email address: ... We respect your privacy. View our **privacy policy.** If you believe this has been sent to you in error, please safely **unsubscribe.***

Fab.

Daily Newsletter

Subject:
The Vintage Shop: Iconic Birkin & Kelly Bags By Hermès...

Sent:
2-4 times daily

Content
Vintage products

Fab.

Smile. you're designed to.®

Shop Now ⟩

🌐 Fashion **Tuesday**

Ⓡ *Sale start today at 12:00 CET / 18:00 GMT*

The best part of summer? Dresses. For girls, it's wearing them. For guys, it's watching the girls wear them. Ladies, get sexy with print, leather and vintage-y gowns from **Fleet Collection, vfish, Fairground** and **Alchimie**. Fellas, try to keep your eyes on looking good too with the help of **Han Kjøbenhavn's streetwear**.

Han Kjøbenhavn
Unmistakenly Danish Streetwear

Alchimie
Because The Lady Loves Leather

Fairground
Cool Summer Couture

maxjenny!
Colorful Laptop Cases

Fleet Collection
Vintage-Inspired Summer Dresses

vfish
Flirty Summer Fabrics

📱 **Download the Fab App for your** iPhone, iPad and Android.

About Help Contact Us Return Policy Shipping Terms Privacy

You received this email because you are registered on en.fab.com with the email address: aktenresearchph@gmail.com. We respect your privacy. View our **privacy policy**. If you believe this has been sent to you in error, please safely **unsubscribe**.

Fab.

Daily Newsletter

Subject:
The Fashion Shop: Danish Street Threads, Hot Leather Looks,...

Sent:
2-4 times daily

Content
Fashion products

30 Days To Sell - Converting users from try to buy.

Fab.

Smile, you're designed to®

Shop Now ▶

♥ **Young at Heart Wednesday**

Getting old is really getting old, isn't it? But we can change all that! Tonight, let's reboot your youth with a **Superman** tee, a new monster friend from **Noodoll**, and a critter crossing bag by **out_of_ark**. Light up your bike with **Go & Glow's** LED spoke lights and turn back a kooky clock from **Cuadros Lifestyle.**

Noodoll
Monstrously Cute Accessories

Superman
Man Of Steel Style Appeal

Cuadros Lifestyle
Tick Tock Terrific

out_of_ark
Bags For Wild World Wanderers

Go & Glow
Fix Up, Light Up, Look Sharp

Pleased To Meet
Retro Cool Stationery & Prints

📱 **Download the Fab App for your** iPhone, iPad and Android.

About Help Contact Us Return Policy Shipping Terms Privacy

You received this email because you are registered on us.fab.com with the email address: clawresearchgh@gmail.com. We respect your privacy. View our *privacy policy*. If you believe this has been sent to you in error, please safely **unsubscribe.**

Fab. Fab.com GmbH Phisgestrasse 21-74 3, Hof. 100 10 Berlin
Managing Directors: Jason Goldberg, Nima Malfiani
District Court Charlottenburg: HRB 138601 USt.-Idnr. DE213269811

Daily Newsletter

Subject:
The Young@Heart Shop: Monstrous Accessories, Super Superman Stuff...

Sent:
2-4 times daily

Content
Playful products

Fab.
Smile, you're designed to.

Daily Newsletter

Subject:
The Pets Shop: 3D Animal Mugs, Doggie-At-Sea Lifejackets...

Sent:
2-4 times daily

Content
Pet products

Daily Newsletter

Subject:
3-In-1 Bikes, Bookshelves & Planters Crafted From Upcycled Barrels...

Sent:
2-4 times daily

Content
New products

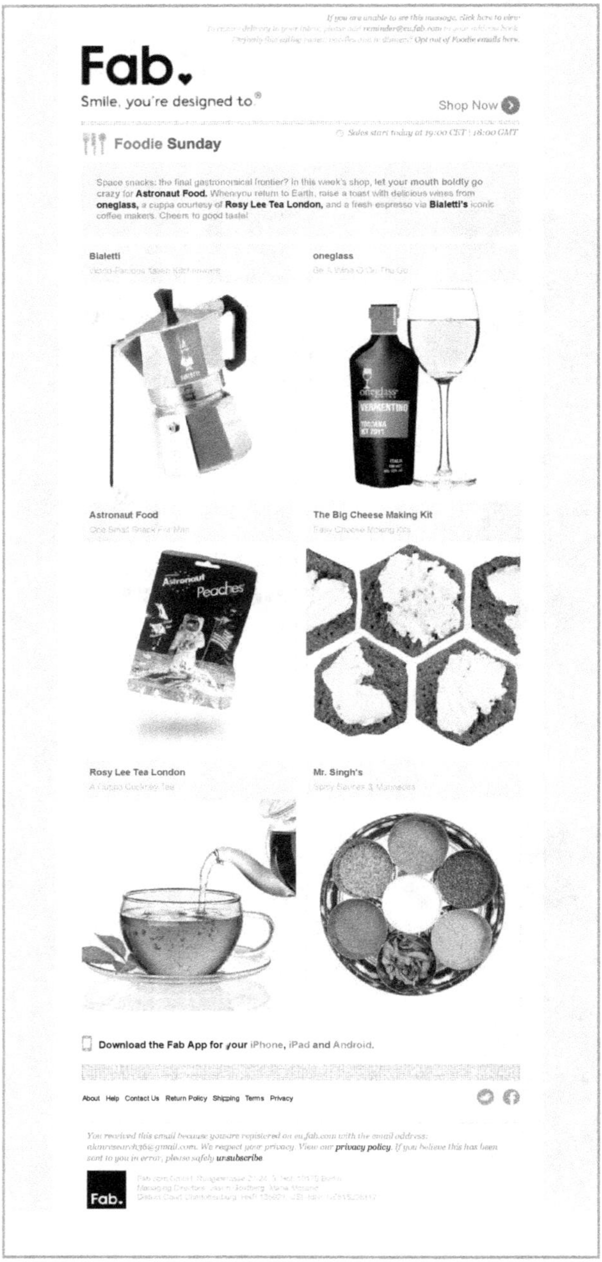

Fab.

Smile, you're designed to.

Shop Now ▶

🍴 Foodie **Sunday**

Space snacks: the final gastronomical frontier? In this week's shop, let your mouth boldly go crazy for **Astronaut Food**. When you return to Earth, raise a toast with delicious wines from **oneglass**, a cuppa courtesy of **Rosy Lee Tea London**, and a fresh espresso via **Bialetti's** iconic coffee makers. Cheers to good taste!

Bialetti

oneglass

Astronaut Food

The Big Cheese Making Kit

Rosy Lee Tea London

Mr. Singh's

Download the Fab App for your iPhone, iPad and Android.

About   Help   Contact Us   Return Policy   Shipping   Terms   Privacy

Fab.

Daily Newsletter

Subject:
The Foodie Shop: Kitchenware By Italian Coffee Gods...

Sent:
2-4 times daily

Content
Kitchen products

30 Days To Sell - Converting users from try to buy.

Conclusion

30 days ago, David signed up to try your service. Over the following days;

- You have given him a warm welcome to get him excited
- Step by step, you showed him how to be a product ninja while guiding him through your service.
- You asked what he wanted to do next and were there to support and delight him.
- You found out what he really needed and gave it to him.
- And when he forgot about you, you gave him a gentle, and maybe not so gentle nudge.

You did all this while working and growing other parts of your business because the entire process was automated. Now thats the type of nifty marketing i like.

But what if David still didnt buy?
Well you could always try a prayer...

The hail mary email

At this stage you have nothing to lose. The 30 day trial period is over and the user did not upgrade. Fire off an email or two and see if you can tempt them back.

It may be the case, as we saw with Patrick's customer, that the user just needs a bit of extra time to trial the product. Ask them.

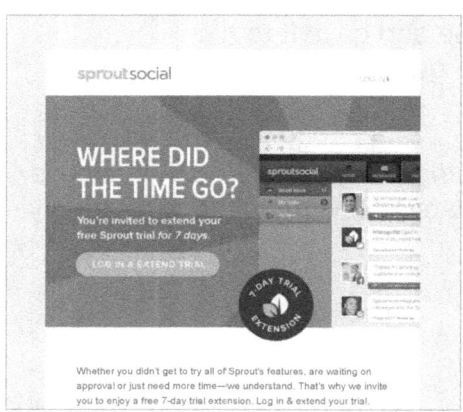 

The price may be too much for other users. But if you are sure the person will not buy at full price, why not offer the product at a reduced price (as long as you will still make a profit on the deal). Or look and see if you can offer another version of the product, reduced in features in some ways.

For some, there is absolutely no substitute to trying the full version of your product. So why not offer a free upgrade trial or a limited offer.

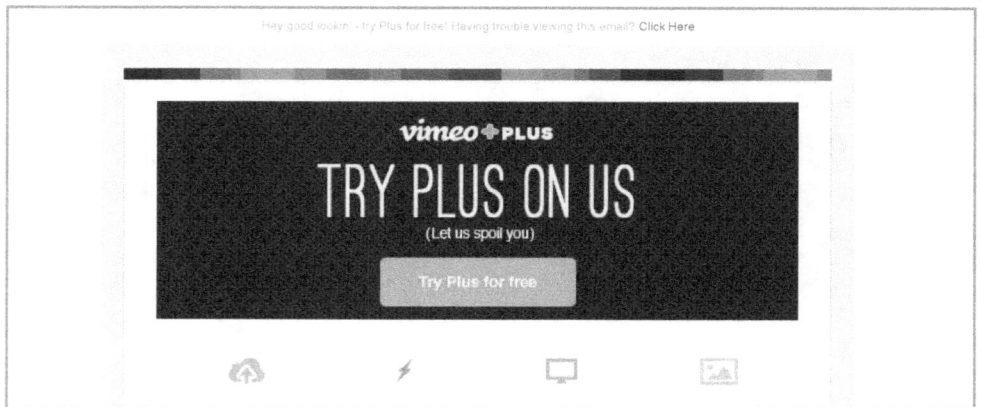

Some users planned to sign up. But on the way to get a cup of coffee, got distracted by a collegue and simply forgot, until your email.

The second opportunity is to get some amazing feedback from the user. Feed the results to your product and marketing teams to improve your product. Tweak the 30 day activation sequence to increase conversion.

Zendesk follow up with the following survey:

```
I'm writing because you have let your Zendesk expire
for this account: trial.zendesk.com. We'd love to
hear your thoughts on how the trial went and what
your plans are. Do any of these reasons match your
situation? Email me with a quick note if you can.
a) I'll be back. My project is on hold.
b) Zendesk is too expensive.
c) I couldn't figure Zendesk out.
d) Went with a different solution (which one?)
e) Zendesk doesn't meet my needs.
f) I did not have enough time to test.
g) Never meant to buy. Was just doing research.
h) Other?
Thanks, Jennifer Hansen
Customer Advocate
```

There is no downside with the hail mary email, only potential upside.

Bonus chapters

Download two bonus chapters. Exclusive for book owners.
http://audiencestack.com/static/book-30-days-to-sell-bonus.html

Marketing Tactics Series

Other books from Alan O'Rourke. http://audiencestack.com/static/books.html

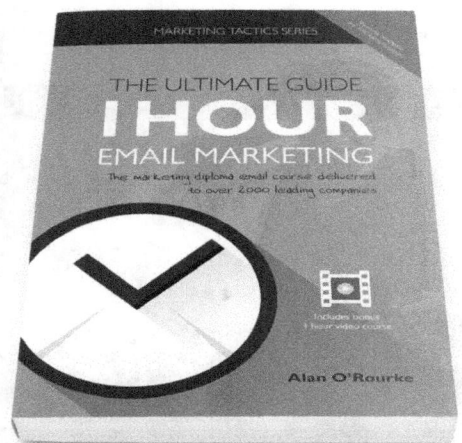

1 hour email marketing
The marketing diploma email course delivered to over 2000 leading companies.

30 days to sell
How the world's leading web sites convert trial users to paying customers.

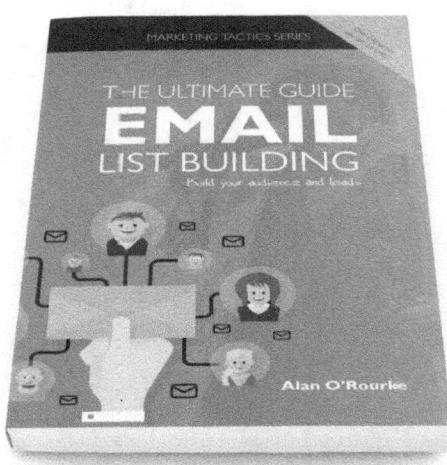

50 monster ideas to get more website links & customers
Tactics to get your website ranking and traffic a boost.

Email list building
Over 200 tactics from leading marketing and sales pros to build your audience and leads.

Beautiful Email Newsletters

Daily inspired email marketing and design at the #1 newsletter gallery showcase on the web.
http://beautiful-email-newsletters.com

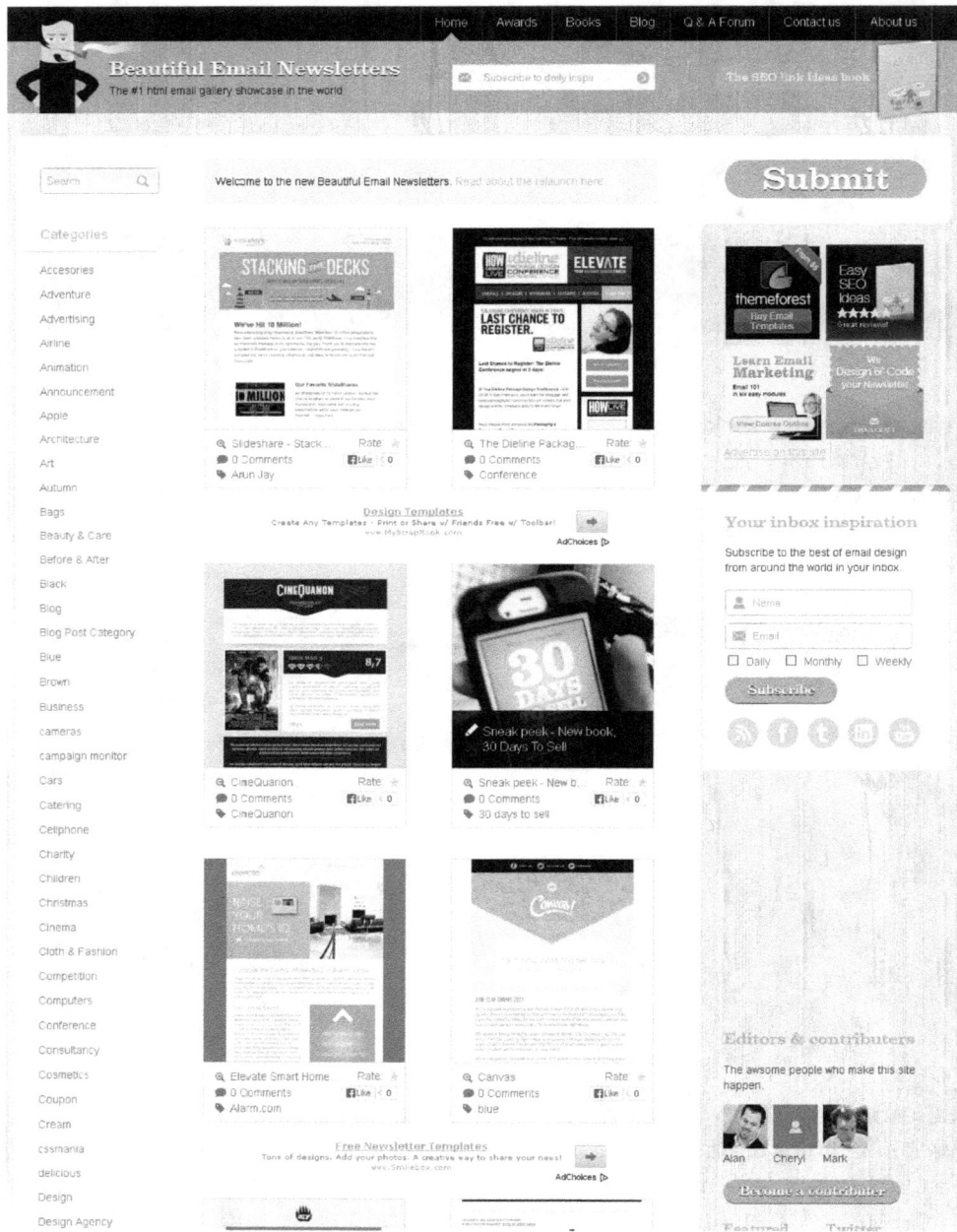

30 Days To Sell - Converting users from try to buy.

50 Monster Ideas
MORE links and Customers

50 link building ideas Google does not want you to know!

This book is designed to provide more actionable items per $ than a typical marketing book.

- Do you need to get your website to the top of Google?
- Is your marketing budget being cut but you still need to bring more customers to your website?
- Do you wish you had a straight forward list of the most effective ways to get first in the search listings?

In this book learn proven ideas to build the profile of businesses big and small all over the world.

Available in Paperback and ebook from Amazon.

http://audiencestack.com/static/book-50-monster-linkbuilding-ideas.html

*****

"This is a practical guide, well written, witty and most of all useful! Actual useful examples of how things work. It really got our creative juices flowing in the office. I honestly can't wait to implement these "
~ Eoin Bara, V7.ie

****

"Nice, easy to read guide that doesn't bombard you with terminology and phrases and instead just covers the facts and shows you how to get on with building links and driving traffic. "
~ Donal Cahalane, smallbusinessrebels.com

About the Author

Alan describes himself as an ex artist, ex film maker, ex designer, ex product manager and ex entrepreneur. He is currently VP of Growth at OnePageCRM.com and author of a few marketing books. One of which you hold in your hands.

Alan was previously a creative director with over ten years of award winning creative strategy, marketing and user engagement design. Author and speaker, Alan previously ran one of Ireland's leading design agencies where he was nominated for a BAFTA award. Alan later founded online marketing software company Toddle. com, building a user base of almost 30,000 users worldwide before selling the company. He is a graduate of business development in DIT but more importantly studied film and he almost made it to the big time as an extra on TV's A Tale At bedtime with Podge and Rodge playing snooker player #2 but they didn't show his good left side.

alan@spoiltchild.com

Linkedin.com/in/spoiltchild

@alanorourke

You can also follow Alan under the alias @ben_approves as he showcases some of the best email designs on www.beautiful-email-newsletters.com

He writes about sales and marketing at http://audiencestack.com

Thank you

A few brilliant people helped me with this book.

Mary Carty, for making me think I could ever write a book and your patience while I did. http://marycarty.com
Eoghan Jennings for making me look at the big picture. https://angel.co/eoghan
Laura Drumgoole and Kat Waitt for making sure what I wrote was real english and made sense. http://lauradrumgoole.com/

www.ingramcontent.com/pod-product-compliance
Lightning Source LLC
Chambersburg PA
CBHW051342170526
45166CB00002B/923